DONAL MURRAY

THE SOUL OF EUROPE

AND OTHER SELECTED WRITINGS

VERITAS

First published 2002 by
Veritas Publications
7/8 Lower Abbey Street
Dublin 1
Ireland
Email publications@veritas.ie
Website www.veritas.ie

ISBN 1 85390 594 1

Copyright © Donal Murray, 2002

The material in this publication is protected by copyright law. Except as may be permitted by law, no part of the material may be reproduced (including by storage in a retrieval system) or transmitted in any form or by any means, adapted, rented or lent without the written permission of the copyright owners. Applications for permissions should be addressed to the publisher.

A catalogue record for this book is available from the British Library.

Cover design by Bill Bolger
Book design and typesetting by Colette Dower
Printed in the Republic of Ireland by Betaprint Ltd, Dublin

Veritas books are printed on paper made from the wood pulp of managed forests. For every tree felled, at least one tree is planted, thereby renewing natural resources.

Contents

Introduction — 5

1. Freedom and the Meaning of Life in Western Europe — 9

2. Poverty, Social Justice and Faith — 21

3. The Role of the Catholic School — 31

4. More than Many Sparrows — 52

5. The Holy Spirit and the Millennium — 71

6. The Soul of Europe — 94

7. To the House of the Father — 101

8. Our Common Vision of Humanity — 116

9.	Youth Ministry– Vision and Practice: A Church Response	131
10.	Signs of Discord, Seeds of Hope	151
11.	Healthcare – Serving Human Life	166

Introduction

In November 1998, almost three years before the attacks on New York and Washington, Peggy Noonan wrote a prophetic article.[1] She reflected that life seems to be full of bustle and stress to a degree that was not the case in the past. Although her life is one of only average intensity, when evening comes, like most people, she finds herself utterly exhausted. We have no time for the really important things. We have no time to think. Perhaps we are afraid to think. We never take time to realise how fragile our world is:

> We fear, down so deep that it hasn't even risen to the point of articulation, that, with all our comforts and amusements, with all our toys and bells and whistles... we wonder if what we really have is... a first-class stateroom on the *Titanic*.

She went on to express her belief that, within a few years, someone would do a 'big terrible thing to New York or Washington'. When that happens, she predicted, 'something tells me that more of us will be praying, and hard...'

It may be that Pope John Paul pointed to the real reason for the failure to think: we are often unable to be silent for fear of meeting ourselves.[2]

The reflections in this book were written over the period of a decade (1992-2001). They address several different issues, from education to bioethics, from social justice to youth ministry, from the nature of freedom to the encyclicals of Pope John Paul, from which almost every chapter draws inspiration.

They were intended for different audiences and different contexts. Although they were not written as a single book, they do, I believe, have a certain coherence. They are reflections on being a Christian in the context of our times. That reflection requires taking time to think, to reflect on our world, to reflect on ourselves.

In his first encyclical Pope John Paul wrote words that are referred to several times in the course of the book. He said that reflection on ourselves in the light of Christ 'bears fruit not only of adoration of God but of deep wonder at [ourselves]... In reality, the name for that deep amazement at human worth and dignity is the Gospel, that is to say, the Good News'.[3]

That reflection is never completed because the love of God for us is inexhaustibly wonderful. That reflection needs to be made anew in each moment in history, each new challenge we face, each individual life. I hope that *The Soul of Europe* may help those who read it to deepen their reflection on some aspects of the amazing worth and dignity that each of us has been given in the life, death and resurrection of Jesus Christ.

✠ Donal Murray
Easter 2002

Notes
1. P. Noonan, 'There is no time, there will be time' in Forbes ASAP, New York, 30 November 1998, reprinted as 'Stay God's Hand', in *The Times*, London, 16 October 2001.
2. cf. Pope John Paul, *Orientale lumen* (1995), 16.
3. Pope John Paul, *Redemptor hominis*, 10.

Freedom and the Meaning of Life in Western Europe[*]

The theme of *freedom* underlies many of the issues that face humanity today. It might be considered under three overlapping headings.

Freedom and the individual
All freedom is, at root, personal freedom. The first step in our reflection, however, is to ask whether this is identical with what we think of as individual autonomy. As one author has suggested, 'at a certain point of history, men became individuals'; they began to feel the 'impulse to write autobiography'; they became to 'live in private rooms'.[1]

Freedom is a personal reality, but it is not a solitary reality. The free self cannot be understood as a sealed, self-contained entity, a monad. The self can be understood only in terms of the relationships in which it comes into existence and the relationships which nurture it, challenge it, inspire it and perhaps threaten it. It is only in relationships that we come to self-understanding and to freedom.

---

[*] First published in *Atheism and Faith*, Vol. XXVII, No. 3 (1992).

These relationships are found above all in the family and in the many groupings and communities in which a person lives.[2] One of the great threats to freedom in our societies at the beginning of the twenty-first century is the diminished importance with which these communities 'on a human scale' are viewed. The processes which shape our societies

> ...have focused relentlessly on two entities: the individual detached from historical context and the universal, politically realised in the secular state. They have left little space for that third essential component of our social ecology: particular and concrete communities of character, of which religions were and are the most potent examples. To put it briefly and bluntly, neither the individual nor the state is where we discover who we are and why.[3]

The individual in the contemporary sense sees the 'private room' as his or her natural habitat. It is seen as the setting where one is most truly oneself. That 'private room' is a lonely place. It is also a place where individuals can feel overwhelmed by the forces that press in upon them. The paradox is that the characteristic attitude of the isolated individual in the face of political structures and economic forces is not one of freedom, but of helplessness.

The moral approach that corresponds to the notion of individual autonomy is one based on the supreme value of being true to oneself. Any other moral consideration is at best a corollary of this central virtue of sincerity or integrity. This is the view expressed by Polonius in Shakespeare's *Hamlet*:

> This above all, to thine own self be true
> And it doth follow as the night the day,
> Thou canst not then be false to any man.

On reflection, however, we must ask whether it is enough to regard being true to others simply as a consequence of being true to oneself. Is it not rather the case that being true to others is the very meaning of being true to oneself? The anthropology of Vatican II indicates a deeper understanding of what it means to be true to oneself. The human being can discover his or her true self only by the sincere gift of self;[4] the human person can neither live nor develop without relationships with others.[5]

Sincerity, integrity, authenticity are indeed central moral concepts. But one cannot be true to oneself unless one is conscious of the richness of the self and of the relationships within which it lives and develops. In that light we can begin to see that,

> ... integrity is nothing other than the perfection of love ... Integrity goes with the surrender of self.[6]

It is in the context of the family and of other groupings 'on a human scale' that a genuine sense of the relationship between morality and freedom is found. There, within relationships, which are seen and valued as personal, one can discover moral obligations that are not a mere 'having to' but a 'wanting to'. The demands of personal love offer no violence to freedom.[7] This is a morality that cannot be understood in terms of an isolated individual sealed off from human contact. That is why Vatican II saw the family as 'a school for human enrichment'[8] and as 'the principal school of the social virtues which are necessary to every society'.[9]

This deepening of the idea of sincerity opens up the question of faith in God.

1. It does so first of all because the very self to whom we seek to be true is not an isolated monad, but a person

who lives and develops through love. We are most truly ourselves not when we are isolated and alone, but in our relationships. If that is the foundation of our freedom, we cannot escape the question of the ultimate fate of those we love, and indeed of ourselves: 'To love a being is to say you, you in particular, will never die'.[10]

2. It raises the question of faith in God because the love which is the very meaning of integrity is never fully satisfied: '... all human love is finally a longing for God. Only God can give that timeless happiness, that perfect satisfaction, that unchanging lovableness, that unfailing faithfulness which men and women are seeking in one another's love, but cannot fully find there'.[11]

3. It raises the question of faith in God because of the loneliness and the helplessness which characterise existence in private rooms. The scriptural revelation speaks very directly to that loneliness: 'I have called you by your name, you are mine ... Do not be afraid, for I am with you' (Is 43:1, 5). That calling by name reveals the truth about ourselves. The reality of God reveals the mystery of humanity.

Even in the most private room we are never alone: 'When you pray, go to your private room ... and so pray to your Father who is in that secret place' (Mt 6:6). We do not adequately understand who we are unless we know that we are addressed by God. This sense of being in the presence of God is by no means as rare as we might fear. The most recent, as yet unpublished, data from the European Values Systems Survey (1990), indicate that between 58.6% (France) and 86.2% (Northern Ireland) of Catholics take some moments of prayer or meditation. Between 45.6% (West Germany) and 84.9% (Republic of Ireland) of

Catholics indicate that they derive comfort and strength from their religion.

The human person is really free, really escapes from alienation, only by transcending him or herself, and by living the experience of self-giving and of the formation of authentic community oriented towards God, our final destiny.[12]

Freedom and pluralism

All freedom is reciprocal. It is 'not merely a right that one claims for oneself. It is also a duty that one undertakes with regard to others'.[13]

One of the most commonly expressed values of the societies of Western Europe is that of respect for the freedom and convictions of other people. Often, however, the call for tolerance and pluralism does not genuinely penetrate the wall of the 'private room'. The views of others are respected only 'from a distance'. They are respected not in any active or positive sense, but rather on the basis that what a person believes and values is a purely private matter, of no legitimate interest to anybody else.

The strange thing is that such an attitude appears in practice to produce a kind of polarisation and bitterness which are very contrary to the intended result.

One reason for this is obvious. An attitude of merely passive acceptance – 'Your beliefs, whatever they may be, are no business of mine' – does not encourage, or even permit, differing moral standpoints to understand one another. This is particularly the case when, as one finds in our societies, the differences are based on incompatible moral philosophies. There is a profound incompatibility between moral philosophies which relativise all moral norms and those which see the moral search as a search for objective truth. These are differences not just in the conclusions but in the first principles:

> Once we lose a common language, we enter the public domain as competing interest groups rather than as joint architects of a shared society... At its extreme [this environment] produces a clash of fundamentalisms, some liberal, some conservative, neither with the resources to understand the other.[14]

Another reason for the failure of this passive tolerance to produce harmony in society is that it is not sufficient to say to another person. 'It does not matter to me what you believe'. The fact is that a person's beliefs may well matter very greatly to him or her.

A failure to appreciate the importance of another person's beliefs and values is a failure to appreciate myself:

> ... the strange thing is that the more the person I speak to is perceived as extrinsic to me, the more I am at the same time and in the same measure extrinsic to myself; face to face with an anonymous individual, I become myself anonymous, if not literally no longer a person.[15]

Reflection on the respect due to the moral convictions of others raises the question of faith in God in a number of ways:

1. It raises the question of the source of the unconditional nature of moral obligation. This unconditionality is the reason why the moral convictions of others command respect. Can this be explained in terms of the demands made upon me by other people if these other people are understood as mere passing sparks of consciousness in an absurd universe? Can the desire to build a better world for the sake of some remote posterity really be a foundation for the kind of moral commitment which we respect and honour?

> We do not love these men of the future keenly enough; and we love them perhaps the less the more we hear of their evolutionised perfection, their high average longevity and education, their freedom from war and crime ... This is all too finite ... It lacks the note of infinitude and mystery ...[16]

The mystery of the human person and of the human person's search for truth points towards the Absolute, towards the mystery of God; that is ultimately why the moral quest of others demands our respect:

> The guarantee that objective truth exists is found in God, who is Absolute Truth; objectively speaking, the search for truth and the search for God are one and the same.[17]

2. It raises the question of whether it is sufficient to look on the quest for moral truth as a private manner. If we are in any sense to be the 'joint architects of a shared society', it cannot be enough to accept that everybody has a different point of view. If we are to work together toward a common goal, then we must have some shared vision and values. A moment's reflection, however, shows that a shared goal which could fulfil the hopes of all the different people in all the various cultures and from all the range of history is beyond our capacity to create or imagine. If the moral quest is to justify the seriousness which we recognise in it – if it is to be more than the pursuit of an illusion – then it is a search for God, who alone can satisfy the human quest:

> The vigilant and active expectation of the coming of the Kingdom is also the expectation of a finally perfect justice for the living and the dead, for people of all

times and places, a justice which Jesus Christ, installed as supreme Judge, will establish ... In fact, without the resurrection of the dead and the Lord's judgement, there is no justice in the full sense of the term. The promise of the resurrection is freely made to meet the desire of true justice dwelling in the human heart.[18]

Freedom and the world
The idea of human freedom which often appears in an unreflected way in the modern mind is one that is properly verified only in God – the idea of a freedom that is omnipotent, unconditioned and infinite. Freedom is seen as the ability to do anything one wishes, to bring about any situation one desires. Any limitation on that ability is experienced as an obstacle to freedom.

The fact is, however, that our freedom does not operate in a universe in which we are supreme and untrammelled. It is not the ability to create one's own universe: it is the power to deal realistically with the universe that exists. We are free only in a situation, with the possibilities which that situation offers, using the resources which are present or capable of being developed. 'To will is not to create' ['*Vouloir n'est pas créer*'].[19] We live in a world which we did not create, a world whose laws are not subject to unlimited manipulation. We share that world with others whose free decisions affect the environment in which we act.

The idea of freedom that would see the world merely as hostile material to be fought or as an obstacle to be overcome misses the point. The fact that we cannot walk through solid walls does not make us less free – we would be less free if we persisted in trying to do so! The really free action is frequently not the one that fights the environment, but the one that best understands and respects it. The great artist, or athlete, or writer does not give the impression of struggling with his or her material but of being entirely at home in it. The true genius 'makes it look easy'.

A particularly important aspect of the need to respect and understand the world in which we exercise our freedom is inescapably posed by the ecological question:

> ... the increasing devastation of the world of nature is apparent to all. It results from the behaviour of people who show a callous disregard for the hidden, yet perceivable requirements of the order and harmony which govern nature itself.[20]

One aspect of the world which the free action has to respect is the past. The illusion of a freedom which would be unlimited would regard the past, the tradition, as a limitation. It is a mistake described by T. S. Eliot over 70 years ago, when he pointed to:

> ... our tendency to insist, when we praise a poet, upon those aspects of his work in which he least resembles anyone else. In these aspects or parts of his work we pretend to find what is individual, the peculiar essence of the man ... Whereas if we approach a poet without this prejudice we shall often find that not only the best, but the most individual parts of his work may be those in which the dead poets, his ancestors, assert their immortality most vigorously.[21]

The realisation that freedom is situated in time and must deal with the physical world points to the question of faith in God.

1. All freedom begins with an act of consent. This is not a surrender, but a recognition that the actual world is the arena within which one is free:

To consent is not a surrender if despite appearances the world is the possible theatre of freedom. I say: here's my place, I adopt it; I will not yield, I acquiesce; it's good here; because 'all things work together for good for those who love God, who are called according to his purpose'.[22]

Consent to the limited nature of the universe in which we live and act is further opened up by hope. Hope recognises that while the world is 'the possible theatre of freedom', it is not the definitive homeland of freedom: 'I consent to the extent that I am able, yet I hope to be delivered from awfulness'[23]. This raises the question of the ground of that hope of deliverance and of the justification for regarding the universe to which we consent as reasonable and as benign. Once again we are faced with the question of faith in God.

2. It is impossible to act freely while ignoring one's history and tradition. That is not to say that one must accept that tradition uncritically; it does mean, however, that wherever one wishes to go in life, one must begin from where one has now arrived.

The Christian tradition which has formed the culture of Western Europe may appear to be in decline. On the other hand, in the European Values Survey,[24] it appeared that the Churches were regarded with greater confidence than the Press, the trades unions and the political parties.

Christian revelation is far from being a limitation of freedom. It is the promise that the effort to build a true unity of the human family is not in vain;[25] it is the Good News which results in a 'deep amazement at human worth and dignity',[26] it is a call to avoid:

> ... every kind of illusory freedom, every superficial unilateral freedom, every freedom that fails to enter into the whole truth about humanity and about the world.[27]

The Christian Gospel points to a freedom which recognises that there is more to the human person than the shallow, autonomous individual who appears in the first superficial glance of self-reflection. As Karl Rahner pointed out, in the last judgement we shall see the truth about ourselves and, what is more, we shall realise that this was a truth that we always knew!

The Christian Gospel shows us that we exercise our freedom as creatures, in a world which is not made by us. If we seek to ignore the plan of the Creator, then we provoke disorder which disrupts the harmony between ourselves and God, ourselves and others, ourselves and the world. Freedom only operates by dealing with a reality that it does not create.

The freedom that is at the heart of the Gospel message, that is the fruit of the Gospel truth, in the universe in which we live, is that:

> Jesus Christ meets the human being of every age, including our own, with the same words: 'You will know the truth and the truth will make you free' (Jn 8:32).[28]

Notes

1. L. Trilling, *Sincerity and Authenticity*, Oxford University Press, 1974, pp. 24, 25.
2. cf. Pope John Paul II, *Centesimus annus*, 49.
3. J. Sacks, *The Persistence of Faith*, Weidenfeld and Nicolson, 1991, p. 14.
4. cf. Vatican II, *Gaudium et spes*, 24.
5. cf. *Gaudium et spes*, 12.
6. D. Connell, *Christian Integrity*, Veritas, 1992, p. 7.
7. Connell, D., loc. cit.
8. *Gaudium et spes*, 52.
9. Vatican II, *Gravissium educationis*, 3.
10. G. Marcel, *Homo viator*, Harper, 1962, p. 147.
11. Bishops of Ireland, *Christian Marriage*, 1969, § 1.
12. cf. *Centesimus annus*, 41.
13. Pope John Paul II, *Message for the World Day of Peace*, 1981.
14. J. Sacks, op. cit. p. 88.
15. G. Marcel, *Essai de Philosophie Concrète*, Gallimard, 1967, p. 55 [my translation].
16. W. James, *Essays on Faith and Morals*, Meridian Books, 1962, p. 212.
17. *Message for the World Day of Peace*.
18. Congregation for the Doctrine of the Faith, *Instruction on Christian Freedom and Liberation*, 60.
19. P. Ricoeur, *Le Volontair et l'involuntaire*, Aubier, 1967, p. 456.
20. *Message for the World Day of Peace*.
21. T. S. Eliot, 'Tradition and the Individual Talent' [1919] in *Selected Essays*, Faber & Faber, 1953, p. 14.
22. P. Ricoeur, op. cit, p. 439 [my translation].
23. Ibid. p. 451
24. M. Fogarty, (ed.), *Irish Values and Attitudes*, Dominican Press, 1984.
25. *Gaudium et spes*, 38.
26. Pope John Paul II, *Redemptor hominis*, 10.
27. ibid, 12.
28. ibid.

Poverty, Social Justice and Faith*

The Voice and the eyes of the poor
On the Southern cotton plantations of the United States, there were, no doubt, some very respectable people, kind to their children, considerate to their aged relatives, honest in business dealings, loyal to their friends, church-goers and bible readers. But all that virtue existed within a lifestyle which required that slaves should be huddled in crude wooden sheds, without a family life, without education, without basic freedoms, in conditions calculated to destroy their self-respect.

One wonders with what kind of deafness and blindness did the slave owner read verses like:

> God listens to the poor
> he has never scorned his captive people. (Ps 69:33)

---

* An address delivered to the European Assembly of the Jesus Caritas Fraternity, August 1991. First published in *The Furrow*, January 1992.

The question that faces us is whether we are living in a kind of Southern plantation while the Lord's poor, the Lord's captive people, are unheard and unseen at our doors.

Pope John Paul speaks of:

> ... the background of gigantic remorse caused by the fact that, side by side with wealthy and surfeited people and societies, living in plenty and ruled by consumerism and pleasure, the same human family contains individuals and groups that are suffering from hunger. There are babies dying from hunger under their mothers' eyes ... It is obvious that a fundamental defect, or rather a series of defects, indeed a defective machinery is at the root of contemporary economics and materialistic civilisation, which does not allow the human family to break free from such radically unjust situations.[1]

That remorse may be focused by reflecting that, in Matthew 25, the Lord's judgment sees the situation through the eyes of the poor and is spoken in the name of the poor: 'I was hungry and thirsty and you did not give me food and drink.'

From the point of view of the relatively secure person, as every priest is in Ireland, it is easy to make what appear to be realistic and reasonable judgments of the situation: 'Great economic advances cannot be made overnight; the struggle to defeat unemployment will be a long haul.' Such statements are true as far as they go: even the best of intentions will be hampered by inadequate resources and by the complexity of the economic situation.

But, however true that may be, such statements provide little consolation to parents whose children are missing educational opportunities that will not recur, or to people who cannot receive health care when they need it, or who have no prospect of getting a job. They will not be impressed with our confident hope of better things for their grandchildren.

There are real obstacles in the way of a solution; these cannot simply be ignored. Precisely because the effects of poverty are so unacceptable, it is important to avoid the trap of pursuing well-meaning but ill-informed steps, which, in spite of the real concern which fuels them, simply make the situation worse.

It remains true that only what Dean Swift's epitaph called *saeva indignatio*, a blazing indignation, undiluted by rationalisation, by selfishness, or by the kind of excuses which sound weak and unacceptable to deprived people themselves can fuel the kind of resolve that the situation demands. Such indignation can come only from listening to, and as far as possibly sharing, the pain that poverty brings. That is the first thing that our reflection indicates: we need the conversion, the *metanoia*, which comes from seeing reality as it is seen by the Lord. He sees it with the eyes of the poor and passes judgment on it with the voice of the poor.

The dignity of the person
This is, in itself, a deep and uncomfortable challenge, but it is not the whole picture. When one looks around this country and sees the high levels of unemployment and emigration, one is rightly outraged at the economic disadvantages that people suffer. One can begin to think of the defective machinery simply in terms of the workings of the economy. The Pope's phrase was much wider: 'a defective machinery is at the root of contemporary economics and materialistic civilisation'.[2] The issue is not purely economic: it has to do with the values underlying our civilisation.

In a society where social standing is largely measured in terms of job and income, poverty and unemployment attack a person's self-esteem. They place a strain on relationships in the family and in the extended family – parents feeling that they are failing their children, children embarrassed at the low standing of their parents, lack of understanding from in-laws and neighbours. Poor people often feel excluded from participation in social and cultural life, and even from voluntary and community activities – often involving hidden costs which others scarcely notice but which may be prohibitive for people who are poor.

Poverty is an obstacle to the full development of people as people. It can be an obstacle to spiritual development. Some of the basic building blocks of relationship with God are attitudes like hope, thanksgiving, a knowledge of being loved by God. These can pose particular problems for someone who is poor in modern society. No doubt some people do come to these religious attitudes with a new depth from a situation of poverty – it is hardly necessary to say that to followers of Charles de Foucauld! At the same time, the challenge of coming to know God's love in that situation should not be underestimated.

Perhaps the greatest spiritual difficulty here in Ireland is that the community from which poor people feel alienated and excluded, the community in which these false criteria and values are visible is, overwhelmingly, made up of the very people who are called to be the sacrament of God's presence in the world, the Body of Christ in which people should be able to recognise God's unconditional love for them.

The discovery of that dignity in the lives of those who are poor is their greatest challenge. It is an even more radical challenge for those who are not poor. It is a challenge particularly for us priests – part of a society that marginalises and diminishes the poor, yet preachers of a gospel that proclaims them to be especially blessed and of a social teaching that has as a constant theme:

the option, or love of preference for the poor. This is an option, or a special form of primacy in the exercise of Christian charity, to which the whole tradition of the Church bears witness.[3]

The challenge facing Europe

We in Europe are in a process of dramatic and unpredictable change. The changes in the formerly Communist states of Eastern Europe, in what was the Soviet Union, and the development of the Single Market – these will alter the face of the continent in ways that we cannot foresee.

The issues of poverty and social justice highlight the question that is at the core of the challenge facing Europe. It is at the core of the ministry and of the whole of the social teaching of the Church:

> ... the main thread and, in a certain sense, the guiding principle of Pope Leo's Encyclical [*Rerum novarum*], and of all the Church's social doctrine, is a correct view of the human person and of the human person's unique value ...[4]

In *Centesimus annus*, Pope John Paul spoke of the alienation that existed in the Communist states. It arose from the violation of rights, from the denial of freedom and responsibility and from the attempt to suppress the question of God. He spoke about alienation in the West as a result of consumerism 'when people are ensnared in a web of false and superficial gratification rather than being helped to experience their personhood in an authentic and concrete way'.[5]

Poverty and other forms of social injustice are powerful sources of alienation. That is the great evil they do: they deny and undermine the dignity of the person.

Alienation means simply this: that people lose sight of their own true value. It is the product of an understanding and a social system that do not adequately appreciate the dignity and destiny of the human person.

There is a superficiality about Western society. One can see it reflected in a tendency to regard society merely as an economy, to see morality as a mere collection of rules, conventions or feelings, and to look on the Church as a mere institution. The appreciation of the richness of social living, the realisation that morality is about recognising and fostering human life, potential and relationships, the understanding of the Church as a shared life in Christ are in danger of disappearing from people's minds until nothing is left of these realities but the dead shell. This impoverishment reflects a failure to understand the deep reality and the dignity of the person. That is why Pope John Paul said to the bishops of Europe in 1985:

> The Church is called to give soul to modern society...[6]

His first encyclical is prophetic when it speaks of the link between the gospel and the dignity of the human person, placing the value of the person at the very centre of what happens when we assimilate the reality of the Incarnation and Redemption – we learn to adore God and, at the same time, to wonder at ourselves:

> In reality, the name for that deep amazement at human worth and dignity is the Gospel, that is to say, the Good News. It is also called Christianity. This amazement determines the Church's mission in the world and, perhaps even more so, 'in the modern world'.[7]

Poverty and social injustice are symptoms of the shallowness which loses sight of that wonder at the dignity of the person. The lack of a burning sense of indignation about poverty and injustice arises from a failure really to recognise those who are poor and to listen to them. That is the importance of the Christian virtue of solidarity:

> Solidarity helps us to see the 'other' – whether person, people or nation – not just as some kind of instrument, with a work capacity and physical strength to the exploited at low cost and then discarded when no longer useful, but as our 'neighbour', a helper (cf. Gen 2:18-20) to be made a sharer, on a par with ourselves, in the banquet of life to which all are equally invited by God.[8]

Listening with the poor

The voice of the poor person is the voice that calls us to repent. It proclaims the hope of a peace that the world cannot give and a justice that 'surpasses all human possibilities' and that brings an answer to the 'immense load of suffering borne by all the generations'.[9]

The voice of the poor tells us that our hopes are too small. Our ideas of peace and justice fall short of the truth that sets us free. They do not offer an answer to the immense load of suffering borne by all the generations. They do not even offer an answer to the immense load of suffering borne by this generation. With every moment that passes, babies die of starvation in their mothers' arms; people die without ever having had proper healthcare and education. The peace and justice that offer satisfaction for all that suffering is not of our puny construction. If we listen to the Good News with those who are poor, we hear a promise that is infinitely greater than the petty ambitions of those of us who may feel that our goods are safely gathered into barns!

We preach that 'here the body of a new human family grows, foreshadowing in some way the age which is to come'.[10] But it is a family in which the stratifications and prejudices and discriminations of our world are absent, or, one should say, reversed.

This is an evangelisation that we need as individuals. It is an evangelisation that our communities and parishes need. It is a losing of a small and ultimately impotent vision in order to find the truth that makes us free. It is an evangelisation that occurs when we begin to see ourselves and our world with the pain and with the urgent demand for change, which comes from seeing it through the eyes of the least of our brothers and sisters – who will be the greatest in the kingdom of heaven.

Lifestyle
One of the really crucial things is that we try to see our own lifestyle through the eyes of those who are poor. How far, from their point of view rather than ours, are we part of the materialist world which mocks them by valuing people on a scale where they cannot but rank low – the scale of a world that is 'caught up in the heady enthusiasm of consumerism and pleasure seeking'.[11]

The average priest has an income that gives rather limited scope for the heady enthusiasm of consumerism! Nevertheless our lives would appear as incredibly luxurious to the victims of African famine or to the homeless in our cities. A daily newspaper may cost not far short of four times the per capita GNP of Mozambique.

Nearly fifteen years ago, the Irish bishops said:

> Luxury and waste in our country and in our world are a scandal. They can amount to a social sin.[12]

The question of waste has become especially urgent in

> ... the so-called civilisation of 'consumption' or 'consumerism' which involves so much 'throwing

away' and 'waste'. An object already owned but now superseded by something better is discarded, with no thought of its possible lasting value in itself, nor of some other human being who is poorer.[13]

There is something fundamentally wrong with a society that throws away perfectly good articles which could make a real difference to someone who could never afford to buy them. One might be tempted to add the judgment of Matthew 25, 'I needed something and you threw it away.'

We need to look at our own lifestyle not simply because of the offence it offers to brothers and sisters who are poor, but because we are witnesses to something better. The voice of the poor helps us to discover a lifestyle that reflects the human worth and dignity that are integral to the gospel:

> It is therefore necessary to create life-styles which the quest for truth, beauty, goodness and communion with others for the sake of common growth are the factors which determine consumer choice, savings and investments.[14]

Thoughtless waste is a symptom of that same emptiness, that inability to see anything deeper than the shell, that failure to understand the virtue of solidarity, which is the real threat to Europe and to the world. It is also at the root of the ecological crisis.

Conclusion

The challenge of giving a soul to modern society is the centre of our mission as European priests. One of the key steps in the mission is to listen and see with the poor. If, with them, we hear the voice of God whose salvation is promised not just to the comfortable, the affluent, the respected, but also, and especially, to the downtrodden, the suffering and the neglected, then we begin to repent and believe the Good News.

Then we can believe more deeply and preach more effectively the God who overturns the assumptions on which our societies often operate – the anonymity, the class distinctions, the standards of success and failure. The most important thing about each of us is that we are not anonymous, we have an amazing worth and dignity because the Lord say to us:

> I have redeemed you
> I have called you by your name, you are mine (Is 43:1).
> I know my own and my own know me (Jn 10:14).

They are texts that need to be heard most in the soulless society of consumerism, efficiency and anonymity. But they are texts that are heard in their full richness and power only when they are heard with the most abandoned and neglected people.

Notes
1. Pope John Paul II, *Dives in misercordia*, 11.
2. ibid., 11.
3. Pope John Paul II, *Sollicitudo rei socialis*, 42.
4. Pope John Paul II, *Centesimus annus*, 11.
5. ibid., 41.
6. Pope John Paul II, Address to VI Symposium of CCEE, October 1985.
7. Pope John Paul II, *Redemptor hominis*, 10.
8. *Sollicitudo rei socialis*, 39.
9. CDF Instruction on Christian Freedom and Liberation, 60.
10. Vatican II, *Gaudium et spes*, 39.
11. Pope John Paul II, *Reconciliatio et paenitentia*, 18.
12. *The Work of Justice*, 120.
13. *Sollicitudo rei socialis*, 13.
14. *Centesimus annus*, 14.

THE ROLE OF THE CATHOLIC SCHOOL*

An intense debate on education in Ireland was initiated by the Green Paper, *Education for a Changing World*. The challenge of the changing world was described under a number of headings indicating important considerations of equity, participation, resource allocation and social expectations. Tucked away among these considerations was one of a rather different order: 'The need to educate young people for their role as citizens of Europe, while retaining and strengthening their distinctive Irish identity and culture'.[1]

Here the document touches all too briefly and indirectly on the purpose of education in general and of the school in particular:

---

* First published in *Studies in Education*, vol. II, no. 1, Spring 1995, edited by Daniel Murphy and Valentine Rice, published on behalf of the School of Education by the Department of Higher Education and Educational Research, Trinity College, University of Dublin.

A close examination of the various definitions of school and of new educational trends at every level, leads one to formulate the concept of school as a place of integral formation by means of a systematic and critical assimilation of culture. A school is, therefore, a privileged place in which, through a living encounter with a cultural inheritance, integral formation occurs'.[2]

The greatest challenge facing education is the rapidity of cultural change. What kind of culture will characterise the world in which today's pupils will live most of their lives? What kind of roots will give them nourishment in the unimaginable world of, let us say, the 2030s? What, if anything, is 'their distinctive Irish identity and culture'?

All schools try to meet this challenge in their own way. The Catholic school has a particular role which this article tries to reflect, though much of what is said will apply to other schools.

Odd beyond words
One might begin by considering the role of the Department of Education which produced the Green Paper, directed the subsequent debate, and is soon to propose a White Paper and an Education Act. How far is the state an appropriate vehicle of change in education?

The Chief Rabbi of Great Britain has described what he calls, 'a tenacious modern fallacy: the omnipotence of politics, in the narrow sense of governments, policies and parties. Roughly speaking, this amounts to the view that the political system is the only significant vehicle of change in societies as secular as our own.' Educational policy and standards along with crime, poverty and environmental exploitation, in this view, can be controlled, if at all, only by legislation. But life is more complicated than that: 'The forces that shape a society lie too deep to be reached by any but the most totalitarian political regime ...'[3]

Those forces have to do with people's attitudes to fundamental questions of meaning: What is the purpose of human life? What happens after death? Is there anything worth living for, or dying for? These questions lie at the root of every exercise of human freedom.[4] A society that fails to appreciate this truth is doomed to be superficial; education that is not inspired by an understanding of the meaning of life is shallow.

Frank Sheed pointed out that if education means preparing a human being for life, the state is remarkably unfitted to carry out that task. It cannot answer the fundamental questions: 'What is a human being? What is human life for?' It recognises the variety of answers given by its citizens but cannot, as a political institution, decide among differing philosophies or theologies of life. All education is necessarily based on some answer to those questions, recognised or unrecognised. To undertake the work of education without thinking the questions relevant, 'is odd beyond all words. Yet it does not strike people as odd. And the depths of their unawareness of its oddness is the measure of the decay in thinking about fundamentals'.[5]

One can seek to escape this charge by suggesting that the purpose of education is simply to provide the skills and information that will enable young people to become good citizens. But the same difficulty arises. What is the point of citizenship, or indeed of the state itself, unless it enables people to become more fully and richly human? And how can one speak about full and rich humanity without an answer to the fundamental human questions? A state in which people's ideals rose no higher than the fulfilment of civic duties and an education system which sought to do no more than produce good citizens would be inhuman and dehumanising.

A person is not just a citizen. Citizenship is a role that makes demands in limited areas of life. The state does not control, nor have a claim over, the whole of life.

What then are the implications for the education debate of the principle that everyone seems willing to endorse, namely, that education must seek the development of the whole person? Does it not follow that education should be conducted as far as possible in contexts where a person's fundamental approach to life can be naturally and freely expressed? Should it not take place in a setting that invites parents and pupils to take part with the fullness of their beliefs and with the whole of themselves?

There exists a rich variety of cultural interests, friendships and religious convictions among the people of any modern country. The role of the state is not to control or organise or to judge between these but simply to recognise their importance for the life of society.

These are the spheres in which a person exists not in a limited role or function, not simply in terms of achievements, possessions or usefulness, but as a person, valued for who he or she is. It is not enough, therefore, to educate young people for their role as citizens of Europe. There is, as the Green Paper itself recognises, 'the need to develop an awareness of the European heritage and values that we share ...'[6]

This is the paradox of the modern state: any human society, if it is to function in a human way, requires citizens who possess convictions, form associations, and pursue values that do not find their source in the state and that lie outside the state's competence. Our societies are uncomfortable with any suggestion that religious convictions should influence attitudes to social and political questions. For most people, however, convictions at this level are the source of the personal integrity and the commitment to others without which society would disintegrate.

The Green Paper paid far too little attention to the question of how such convictions can find their proper place in the educational philosophy of Irish schools. Their source is not and cannot be the state.

Who educates?

The basic argument of Rabbi Jonathan Sacks in his Reith Lectures was that:

> The Enlightenment and the intellectual and social processes to which it gave rise have had a devastating effect on the traditions which give meaning and shape to life lived in community. They have focused relentlessly on two entities: the individual, detached from historical context, and the universal, politically realised in the secular state. They have left little space for that third component of our social ecology: particular and concrete communities of character, of which religions were and are the most potent examples. To put it briefly and bluntly, neither the individual nor the state is where we discover who we are and why.[7]

The answer to the question, 'Who educates?', is found neither in the individual nor in the state, but in the particular communities 'where we discover who we are and why'. Education is primarily the task of the 'third component', that is, of 'particular concrete communities' – families, churches, organic natural groupings in which one is accepted as a whole person. This is as distinct from structures, artificial entities coming from the top down. Useful as it may be, a structure exists for limited purposes and is incapable of addressing the deepest questions about the destiny of the whole person.[8]

The alienation that is characteristic of modern society arises largely from the fact that an increasing proportion of life is lived in structures where one fulfils a function rather than in communities where one participates as a whole person.[9] It is vital to restore the role of the 'third component':

> Apart from the family, other intermediate communities exercise primary functions and give life to specific networks of solidarity. These develop as real communities of persons and strengthen the social fabric, preventing society from becoming an anonymous and impersonal mass, as unfortunately often happens today. It is in interrelationships on many levels that a person lives, and that society becomes more 'personalised'.[10]

It is in these 'intermediate communities' that people grow as people. That is where they learn their own worth; that is where they develop the ability to relate to others; that is where their basic moral concepts are formed; that is where they come to their vision of the meaning of life.

The educational dialogue through which a person enters into 'a systematic and critical assimilation of culture' concerns the whole person, because the way in which people are involved in their own cultural formation depends upon their understanding of themselves and of their destiny.[11] If one loses sight of that, one is reduced to an increasingly desperate effort to build into society, and particularly into schools, a system of moral and spiritual education that must be based on a lowest common denominator. Education is left trying to approach the question of how we should live while ignoring the question of what life means and where it leads.

That is why 'intermediate communities', 'particular and concrete communities of character', have to be the moving force in any education worthy of the name. That is why such communities, and this does not refer simply to the Catholic Church and other religious groupings, should be allowed and encouraged to establish and manage schools in which they can share their living vision with young people.

Embarrassment or reluctance about the sharing of convictions risks leading to an idea of education that is pale, uninspiring and alienating. It risks producing an encounter with their cultural inheritance that involves neither the whole person of the students nor the whole of their culture.

Participation in the Catholic school
To ask the question, 'Who educates?', is to raise the issue of participation. The notion that this is necessarily facilitated by bringing education into line with the structures of political administration needs to be approached with scepticism. Political structures exist for clearly defined and limited goals. Giving young people an understanding of the meaning of human life and helping them to develop the values that will inspire them in the third millennium are not among the purposes for which we elect public representatives whether at national or local level.

In any case participation is not simply about structures, it is about having educational milieux into which pupils and parents can enter with the whole of themselves and with the whole of their understanding of life. The purpose of the Catholic school is to be a context in which the Catholic understanding of life is fully lived and fully at home:

> [The Catholic school] no less than other schools pursues the goal of the cultural and human formation of young people. Its characteristic function, however, is to develop in the school community an atmosphere inspired by the gospel spirit of freedom and love and to help young people, while developing their own

individual personality, to grow at the same time in the new creation brought about in them by baptism.[12]

It goes without saying that this describes the goal rather than the reality. Every Catholic school falls short of that goal to a greater or lesser degree.

The function of a Catholic school requires that it be rooted in the wider community of believers:

> Faith is principally assimilated through contact with people whose daily life bears witness to it. Christian faith, in fact, is born and grows inside a community. The community aspect of the Catholic school is necessary because of the nature of the human being and the nature of the educational process which is common to every school. No Catholic school can adequately fulfil its educational role on its own.[13]

This is a particular instance of the general concern among educationalists that the school should be rooted in the real world. The Transition Year, home-school-community liaison, links between schools and industry are all efforts to bridge the gap.

The Catholic school at primary level is usually well rooted in the parish community. At post-primary level there is a great deal to be done in building up a sense of the school as an integral part of the wider Church family. The Catholic community needs to put flesh on its responsibility for the education of its second-level students; the schools themselves need new ways of finding roots and partners in the community. Education is done not by a school alone but by the community of which the school is an organic part.

There is need for a massive effort to grow in understanding of the fact that education in faith, and all education, is a task for which the whole Church and each member must feel responsible.[14] Every school has to be a 'community school'. In the more cohesive community which Ireland was, even in the recent past, such challenges may have seemed to lack urgency. That is no longer the case.

The foundation for efforts to build up a sense of community involvement must be the acceptance of responsibility by the community of which the school is a part. Structures that look good on paper can often diminish rather than increase participation. It may be a mistake to seek the solution in 'the omnipotence of politics'.

There has been considerable change and adaptation in the education system in recent decades. These changes were prompted by perceived needs recognised by the providers of education; they were not the product of legislation. It is important not to bring about a situation in which the law might restrict the ability of schools, teachers, communities and public servants to be responsive to perceived needs in the future.

It has been suggested in the current debate that the Education Act should lay down the numbers and the forms of representation on Boards of Management, while the Churches and other groups that have founded schools would have some kind of legal protection for their ethos. There is every danger that this would be a recipe for making a school less of a community and more of a structure.

More importantly, it is a striking example of what Frank Sheed thought so odd. It turns things on their head. Surely it is the groups of people who establish schools for the education of their children who should decide how those schools are to be run? Surely it is the state that should make legal provision to ensure that the minimum standards, the equity and the efficiency that it requires are achieved?

Underlying much of the thinking in this area is an extraordinary upending of reality: since taxpayers money is being used, the state should, so it is claimed, decide how education is to be run. Parents and the community in general are thus deemed to hand over their money to the state so that it may ensure that their children are educated as it sees fit. The truth is quite the contrary: they pay their taxes so that the state may assist *them* in educating their children as they see fit.

The ethos of a Catholic school

The idea that the ethos of a school could be protected by some legal device is superficially attractive. The trouble with an ethos is that, while it is easy to recognise, it is difficult to define. One could see, at the National Education Convention, the puzzlement and frustration with which people sought to elicit or to express a strict definition of 'ethos'. There is no legally enforceable definition of 'the gospel spirit of freedom and love'. The only way of ensuring that a branch remains alive is that it should continue to be attached to a living tree. If the connection is broken, nothing that one can do can save the branch in the long run.

The ethos of a Catholic school derives from its living contact with a living community of faith. The school is an integral part of the family of believers. From that community the school receives its spirit. The school shares with Catholic parents and with the whole Church in helping students to understand and live the Good News; it is concerned for the life of the Church at home and abroad; it maintains links with parishes and church associations.[15] Through its liturgy and prayer students and staff can express the awe that accompanies all real learning, and can do so in the 'deep amazement' that comes from seeing our lives in the light of the Gospel.[16]

This ethos or religious spirit should pervade the life of the school: 'In a Catholic school, and analogously in every school, God cannot be the Great Absent One or the unwelcome intruder'.[17]

All schools are engaged in a process of assimilation of culture. This must not be mere absorption, it must be a critical dialogue. A good school must be to some extent counter-cultural, recognising and resisting what is unjust or foolish or dehumanising in the surrounding culture. A Catholic school should be especially concerned to resist the assumption that religion should 'know its place'. There is no corner or aspect of life in which God is irrelevant. Either one recognises God as the Creator and Sustainer of the entire universe and all of history, or one does not recognise him as God. In a Catholic school, therefore, 'the Gospel spirit should be evident in a Christian way of thought and life which permeates all facets of the educational climate'.[18]

Instruction and spirit

The 1965 Rules for National Schools make a similar point:

> Of all parts of the school curriculum Religious Instruction is by far the most important, as its subject matter, God's honour and service, includes the proper use of all man's faculties, and affords the most powerful inducements to their proper use. Religious Instruction is, therefore, a fundamental part of the school course, and a religious spirit should inform and vivify the whole work of the school.

The Green Paper and subsequent discussions expressed concern that this, and more recently the promotion of an integrated curriculum, poses a threat to the rights of children whose religious beliefs differ from those of the majority in a school.[19]

One should note, in the first place, the distinction between religious instruction and a religious spirit. The former is 'part of the school course' – a subject with its own textbooks and syllabus; the latter is an atmosphere that should 'inform and vivify' the life of the school.

There is no such thing as a school that lacks an ethos. This might range from a confused atmosphere in which contradictory attitudes are present, unrecognised or unacknowledged, to the idea that human life has no meaning or purpose beyond our present experience, to the Christian vision of Christ as the Truth, the fullest perfection of human life and the Way to ultimate fulfilment.

Where an ethos is expressed and openly acknowledged, the danger of indoctrination is greatly reduced. The most likely source of indoctrination in our society is a kind of woolly secular liberalism which spreads itself by the magnificently simple method of taking its own truth and enlightenment entirely for granted.

It would be a betrayal of the very nature of the gift of faith to seek to coerce or manipulate anyone into accepting it. It is not, of course, impossible that a Catholic school might become involved in proselytism or in imparting a narrow and one-sided outlook, but, 'this can happen only when Christian educators misunderstand the nature and methods of Christian education'.[20]

Respect for the beliefs of others
Some may fear that a Catholic school might lack respect for the convictions of those who do not share the Catholic faith. In fact the Church in recent years has repeatedly stressed the dignity of conscience, not least in education:

> To deny an individual complete freedom of conscience – and in particular the freedom to seek the truth – or to attempt to impose a particular way of seeing the truth, constitutes a violation of that individual's most personal rights ...

Objectively speaking, the search for truth and the search for God are one and the same ...

Hence, in a way consonant with the nature and dignity of the human person and with the law of God, young people should be helped during their years of schooling to discern and to seek the truth, to accept its demands and the limits of authentic freedom, and to respect the right of others to do the same.[21]

Instruction in Catholic faith must involve 'sincere respect in words and deeds' for other communities of faith; it must give 'a correct and fair presentation of the other Churches and ecclesial communities' and it must 'create and foster a true desire for unity'.[22]

One difficulty which has emerged in recent years is that some parents wish to insulate their children from expressions of Catholic belief, or perhaps from expressions of any religious belief.

That wish cannot be met by withdrawing a child from the periods of religious instruction. The problem is insuperable if the objecting family wishes to ensure that, when their children are present, other pupils should be prevented from speaking about the religious aspects of their lives, from making references to what has been studied in religious instruction or describing events in their local parish. Similarly, if they regard the display of religious art and symbols as offensive, there does not appear to be any way in which their wishes can be reconciled with the wishes of Catholic families. If their position is as outlined, what they are seeking is withdrawal not from religious instruction but from the religious atmosphere of the school.

People have, of course, the right to seek to insulate their children from views and attitudes of which they disapprove. If what they disapprove of is the Catholic faith, then it does not seem realistic to expect to achieve such insulation in a Catholic school. So far as is practical, such parents should be facilitated in finding or establishing schools in which their children can feel at home.[23]

The fear of difference
Underlying discussions about denominational education, especially in Ireland, is the perception that educating children separately is divisive. The strange thing is that the more plural society becomes the more people need space to reflect on their own traditions: 'The demand for segregated denominational schools grows rather than diminishes in a pluralist society'.[24]

The belief that 'private' convictions have no place in social life, or that they should be downplayed, contains an inherent contradiction. It is actually quite disrespectful of another person's beliefs to say, 'You are entitled to believe whatever you wish; it is no concern of mine'. Polarisation is not diminished by ignoring the beliefs of others; it is diminished by understanding both traditions better:

> The answer to these difficult questions [of respect and acceptance for people of different traditions] can be found in a thorough education with regard to the respect due to the conscience of others; for example, through a greater knowledge of other cultures and religions, and through a balanced understanding of such diversity as already exists.[25]

Seeing people come to conclusions different from one's own may be a source of tension if one has little understanding, and little desire for understanding, of why they do so. The passive tolerance which is much too polite to express disagreement may hide an unspoken belief that the other is lax, fundamentalist, outdated, amoral or weird:

> In real life the people who are most bigoted are the people who have no convictions at all. The economists of the Manchester school who disagree with socialism take socialism seriously. It is the young man in Bond Street, who does not know what socialism means, much less whether he agrees with it, who is quite certain that these socialist fellows are making a fuss about nothing.[26]

In a modern society people need to be bilingual. If we try to operate simply in terms of what everybody is agreed on, our speech becomes more and more incapable of dealing with what divides us. 'The problem is that pluralism gives rise to deep and intractable conflicts while at the same time undermining the principles by which they might be resolved'.[27] We need to make way for the second, richer languages which express the values that make us what we are:

> Our second languages are cultivated in the context of families and communities, our intermediaries between the individual and the state. They are where we learn who we are; where we develop sentiments of belonging and obligation; where our lives acquire substantive depth. Pluralism should not simply be neutral between values. Rather it must recognise the very specific value of Christians, Muslims, Buddhists, Sikhs, Hindus and Jews growing up in their respective heritages. Traditions are part of our moral ecology and they should be conserved, not dissolved, by education.[28]

Without a well developed understanding of one's own tradition and an honest, respectful interest in the traditions of others, no genuine pluralism can exist. There is only one way to avoid the dangers of fanaticism and bigotry which can be associated with religious and philosophical beliefs, 'and that is to be steeped in philosophy and soaked in religion'.[29]

Modern culture has some difficulty in recognising the difference between making a judgement and being judgmental, between having a conviction and regarding those who do not share it as inferior. In fact, only a person who regards the search for moral and religious truth as a fundamentally important human activity can properly respect the views of others. If it does not matter what you conclude so long as you are sincere, moral concern itself becomes pointless. There is no longer a shared moral language and dialogue about moral truths becomes impossible.[30]

A situation in which people are not steeped in their own tradition and willing to learn about other traditions is a recipe for bitter misunderstanding. On the other hand, honest expression of convictions need not be divisive. A person of deep convictions is happier with someone of equally deep, if different, convictions than with someone who believes that convictions do not matter:

> Love of one's own land no more implies despising other lands than love of one's own mother implies despising other mothers ... The Patriot, regarding love of country as normal, is happiest with foreigners who love their own country as he loves his.[31]

The Catholic tradition, like all the major religious traditions, offers, not least through its schools, an inspiration and a challenge to people to play a full and positive role together with others in building up a just and peaceful society:

> [The Church] encourages the coexistence and, if possible, the co-operation of diverse educational

institutions which will allow young people to be formed by value-judgements based on a specific view of the world and to be trained to take an active part in the construction of a community through which the building of society is promoted.[32]

Tradition and creativity

There may remain a suspicion that a Catholic school is a place where students are offered ready-made answers and where an uncritical attitude of mind is demanded.

Church schools, like schools in general, have benefited greatly from a clearer modern understanding of the importance of the personal development of the pupil and of helping young people to express the meaning and the truth of their experiences: 'Any school which neglects this duty and which offers merely pre-cast conclusions hinders the personal development of its pupils'.[33]

The truth on which Catholic education is built is not a pre-cast conclusion, it is the infinite God's revelation of himself in his Son. Far from a pre-cast conclusion, it is a truth that we can never fully grasp and that permanently challenges us to open our minds more fully:

> Since our knowledge of God is limited, our language about him is equally so ... God transcends all creatures. We must therefore continually purify our language of everything in it that is limited, image-bound or imperfect, if we are not to confuse our image of God – 'the inexpressible, the incomprehensible, the invisible, the ungraspable' – with our human representations. Our human language always falls short of the mystery of God.[34]

The life of the Church is not a monolithic, unchanging given. It is a living, growing reality:

> Tradition is to be distinguished from the various theological, disciplinary, liturgical or devotional traditions, born in local churches over time. These are the particular forms, adapted to different places and times, in which the great Tradition is expressed. In the light of Tradition, these traditions can be retained, modified or even abandoned under the guidance of the Church's Magisterium.[35]

The Catholic school seeks to be faithful to its Tradition. It is a modern fallacy to think of tradition as the enemy of creativity.[36]

> Ezra Pound's exhortation to 'MAKE IT NEW' hangs over all American culture ... But it is misunderstood. Pound never meant it as a sign that the present erases the past. The phrase fascinated him because he believed that it had been written on the bathtub of the Ch'ing Emperor and that it was an injunction to carry the work of the past, constantly refreshed, into the present: the 'it' is tradition itself.[37]

Affirming our heritage
Many discussions about the future of Irish society suggest that the participants' greatest fear is that Ireland may remain locked in its past. The contrary prospect is more imminent and more dangerous: that Ireland may build its future without valuing our 'distinctive Irish identity and culture'. If the roots are cut, the branch will wither.

Ireland's journey into the future must begin from where we are; it is the continuation of a journey that has a long history. The reflection of the Catholic community on the meaning of that journey, and of how God has spoken to our predecessors in many cultures through that journey, forms the ethos of the Catholic school. The culture and identity derived from our religious traditions and our historical, family and personal experiences are assimilated, systematically but critically.

The pluralist society to which everybody pays lip service surely cannot be one in which these traditions are devalued, or in which people feel that their deepest beliefs should not intrude into public life. It has to be a society that values the variety of traditions and philosophies that make up the multistranded tapestry of Irish life. It has to be a society that understands that people are motivated and inspired by something deeper than the immediate and the visible.

The education system of such a society cannot be one in which everything about which people differ is evened out or declared irrelevant. It has to be one in which the widest provision is made for addressing the whole person in an atmosphere where the pupil can express his or her beliefs without embarrassment.

The Catholic school is the principal way in which Catholic parents and the Catholic community have tried to provide such an education for Catholic children. There are other ways. The Vocational system has, through the years, provided Catholic and other pupils with an education that respected and fostered their beliefs.

In a time of accelerated cultural change, the Catholic school offers an important contribution to a society in danger of cutting its roots. It responds to the need expressed by the Minister at the Education Forum:

> As we respond to altered circumstances and build for the future, we build on the strengths of an education system which has earned the confidence of the Irish people. To retain this confidence, our system must adapt to the challenges of the future. But in facing these challenges we must recognise, value and affirm our cultural and spiritual heritage. If we fail to do this

our education system will lose the characteristics which attune it to the Irish psyche and the Irish spirit.[38]

Notes
1. *Education for a Changing World*, [GP] Green Paper, Stationery Office, 1992, p. 3.
2. *The Catholic School* [CS], Sacred Congregation for Catholic Education 1977, par. 26.
3. Jonathan Sacks, *The Persistence of Faith*, Weidenfeld and Nicolson, 1991, pp. 11, 12.
4. cf. Aquinas, *Summa theologica* I-II q.1, a.6c.; John Paul II, *Veritatis splendor* [VS] 7.
5. Frank Sheed, *Society and Sanity*, Sheed and Ward, 1953, p. 4.
6. GP, p. 86.
7. Sacks, op. cit., p. 14.
8. The school should be seen more as a community than as a structure (institution), cf. *The Religious Dimension of Education in a Catholic School*, [RDECS], Congregation for Catholic Education, 1988, 31.
9. cf. Murray, D., *Can These Bones Live?* Veritas, 1993, and *Life in all its Fullness*, Veritas, 1994.
10. John Paul II, *Centesimus annus* [CA], 49.
11. cf. *CA* 51.
12. Vatican II, *Gravissimum educationis*, 8
13. CS 53, 54.
14. cf. John Paul II, *Catechesi tradendae* [CT] 16.
15. RDECS, 42-44.
16. cf. John Paul II, *Redemptor hominis*, 10; RDECS 111.
17. RDECS 51.
18. RDECS 25. This does not involve any abuse of the autonomy of other subjects on the curriculum, nor any lack of respect for the appropriate methods of teaching these subjects: CS 38, 39.
19. GP pp. 90, 91, *Report on the National Education Convention*, [RNEC] ed. John Coolahan, The National Education Convention Secretariat, 1994, p. 71.
20. CS 19; cf. Vatican II, *Dignitatis humanae* 10; RDECS 6.

21. John Paul II, *Message for the World Day of Peace 1991*, cf. VS 57.
22. CT 32.
23. cf. RNEC, pp. 31-33.
24. Sacks, op. cit., p. 65.
25. Pope John Paul II, *Message for the World Day of Peace 1991*.
26. Chesterton, G. K., *Heretics*, ch. XX, in *Collected Works* vol. I, Ignatius Press, 1986, p. 201.
27. Sacks, op. cit., p. 64.
28. ibid., pp. 66, 67.
29. Chesterton, op. cit., p. 203.
30. cf. Sacks, op. cit., pp. 43ff.
31. Sheed, op. cit., p. 151.
32. CS 13.
33. CS 27.
34. *Catechism of the Catholic Church* [CCC] 40, 42.
35. ibid., 83.
36. See T. S. Eliot, 'Tradition and the Individual Talent' [1919], published in *Selected Essays*, Faber and Faber, 1953.
37. Hughes, Robert, *Culture of Complaint*, Oxford University Press 1993, p, 110.
38. Bhreathnach, Niamh, T. D., *Opening Address*, RNEC, p. 217.

MORE THAN MANY SPARROWS

REFLECTIONS ON EVANGELIUM VITAE[*]

The Gospel of Life
In his first encyclical, *Redemptor hominis*, Pope John Paul used a remarkable phrase. He was talking about the need to reflect on ourselves and who we are in the light of the incarnation and redemption. If we do that, he said, the result is not only adoration of God but wonder at ourselves. And he went on:

> In reality, the name for that deep amazement at human worth and dignity is the Gospel, that is to say: the Good News. It is also called Christianity.[1]

What is unusual about that statement is that it describes Christianity and the Gospel not in terms of what they reveal about God, but rather in terms of what they reveal about humanity. Christianity is the name for that amazement at ourselves! The phrase suggests, in fact, that in presenting

---

[*] An address delivered at Salford on 25 February 1997.

the Gospel, the Good News, to the world today we need to put a strong focus on the vision that it presents of human life. That suggested approach is to be found again and again in what the Pope says and writes, not least in the encyclical *Evangelium vitae*, [The Gospel of Life] published two years ago.

The world says to us, 'Be yourself! Do your own thing!'. The Gospel says, 'Be your *whole* self! Know who you really are!'

We should reflect on why that perspective is so crucial for the world of today and on how it might help us to understand ourselves more fully. In section 81 of *Evangelium vitae* the Pope makes five points about what he calls the Gospel of life:

- It proclaims that the living God is close to us, that he calls us to a deep and intimate relationship with himself and that he awakens in us the sure hope of eternal life.

- It affirms the inseparable connection between a person and their own bodiliness.

- It presents human life as a life of relationship, a gift of God, the fruit and sign of his love.

- It proclaims that Jesus has a unique relationship with every person and that this enables us to see in every human face the face of Christ.

- It calls for a 'sincere gift of self' as the fullest way to realise our personal freedom.

The Transcendent God
The first and most basic thing that the contemporary world – and we ourselves – need to hear and to reflect on is that

the living God is close to us and awakens in us the hope of eternal life.

It is instructive to think about the number of contexts in modern society where that kind of thought would seem embarrassing or out of place. One can hardly imagine anybody in a parliament or a board room or on a factory floor taking time to point out that the infinite God is close to us or that the most important question about some decision we are about to make or some action we are considering is whether it leads us closer to the eternal life God promises.

Why should we be surprised that there is so much alienation from politics and from work? These are areas where most of our time and energy is spent and yet they are contexts where it would seem inappropriate to mention the most fundamental questions about us. What effect does this have on how we see ourselves and how we see our involvement in these areas of life? It says something like, 'Participate, but not with your whole self.' This produces an uneasy feeling that 'there is more to me than this'.

In many areas of life we are expected to behave in a way that suggests that our deepest beliefs and questions are irrelevant. In most situations people would regard it as very impolite to suggest that they had the slightest interest in whether our lives are simply snuffed out at death or whether we will live forever. But surely that must have some impact on how they view us and how they treat us – as sparks of consciousness that flare briefly and disappear, or as beings who will be at home with the eternal God for ever!

The strange thing is that our culture is full of indications that people are searching for something deeper. A programme like *The X-Files* exercises a huge fascination because it is full of mysteries and conspiracies and alien beings and supernatural phenomena. The various series of Star Trek have their devoted followers, who call themselves 'Trekkies'. Many people believe that extraterrestrial beings have visited the Earth in UFOs and landed in Roswell and other places – mostly, it seems, in the United States – they believe that in some cases people have been abducted by aliens and later returned to earth, and that the authorities are suppressing the truth. All sorts of cures and therapies and techniques, which appear to have no scientific basis, attract enthusiastic believers. In this age of science and technology, there is as much superstition as there has ever been. Underlying it all is the unquenchable sense that there is more to life than appears on the surface.

We are perpetually restless because we can see that what goes on in parliaments and boardrooms and in our day-to-day lives is not in itself enough to satisfy us; it is not where we look to find the meaning of our existence. When we look at things rationally, we can see that neither does the answer lie in UFOs or in strange superstitions.

The relatively harmless response to the suggestion of a mysterious meaning as expressed in something like *The X-Files* is one thing. The search to make sense of life through drugs and alcohol, through sexual experience without personal commitment, through the urge to acquire wealth and property for their own sake, through various cults, is not only illusory but can be self-destructive.

The trouble about all these searches is that anything that they may yield is never enough; it never satisfies. No amount of money or drugs or sex or mysterious phenomena will calm the restlessness of the human heart.

Christianity, the Good News, says that this search for meaning is no illusion. It goes further and says that Jesus gives an answer that satisfies all the deepest human questions more fully than we could have imagined. That is why, as the Pope puts it,

> The Church knows that this Gospel of life which she has received from her Lord, has a profound and

> persuasive echo in the heart of every person – believer and non-believer alike – because it marvellously fulfils all the heart's expectations while infinitely surpassing them.[2]

The most fundamental reason why this Gospel echoes in the heart of every person is that,

> we who have the first fruits of the Spirit ... are groaning within ourselves, waiting with eagerness for our bodies to be set free ... And as well as this, the Spirit comes to help us in our weakness, for, when we do not know how to pray properly, then the Spirit personally makes our petitions for us in groans that cannot be put into words (Rom 8:23, 26).

God is close to us, his Spirit is in our hearts, inviting us into communion with himself and into endlessly joyful life. That is the ultimate purpose of our existence, what we are created and redeemed for. That is why we are worth more than many sparrows. Is it any wonder that nothing on earth can fully satisfy us?

To understand that is to understand the real dignity of human beings and the real significance of human life. Life is not just about work or about the organisation of society. The issues that fill the newspapers and the discussion programmes are not where we look to understand who we really are. There is more to us than our work, than our role as citizens, than the concerns that fill our days.

There are other, more profound ways of seeking for meaning. In artistic creativity and self-expression, for instance. Even more significantly, we find meaning in our relationships and our commitments to other people. But the complete answer to the question about the meaning of life is not to be found there either – what we find rather are the questions that open our minds to that meaning. Our creativity will eventually be diminished by illness; our self-expression and our friendships will be broken by death. Indeed, the death of those we love poses the question of meaning in its most telling form. Something within us protests at the idea that death could simply be the end. What we are seeking is more than just a promise of fulfilment for a time. The Gospel tells us that life is the place where we meet the God who created the universe and where we are invited to become his friends for ever.

The message that the world needs to hear is that our restlessness is not something to be ignored or suppressed. There is a temptation nowadays to imagine that the restlessness of the human heart is a question without an answer. The tendency is to tame and domesticate religion. It is something to be laughed at in a comedy programme or to be put on the same plane as politics in discussions about the same old issues, celibacy, contraception, women priests and so on. What must not be allowed to happen, it seems, is that the real questions which religion addresses – about the meaning of life and death, about tragedy, about our unlimited longings for truth and beauty and justice – should be allowed to 'intrude'. Why are we afraid to meet our whole selves?

We believe that the answer is in Christ and that we need to savour that answer and reflect on it. We need to understand that our restlessness is the expression in us of the fact that God is close to us, God is deep within us. As Father Ronald Rolheiser put it: 'At the heart of everything there is a divine fire. In the end, all yearning, longing and aching, every desire we have, is driven by that fire'.[3]

The embodied person
Seeing human beings in the light of that truth gives rise to a sense of reverence, or, to use the Pope's phrase, of 'deep

amazement'. That reverence is not simply something spiritual and ethereal. That is why the second point he makes in section 81 of *Evangelium vitae* is so important. The Gospel of life affirms the inseparable connection between a person and their own bodiliness.

The fact that we are embodied is what gives our 'yearning, longing and aching' its particular tone. The fact that we are embodied means that we are mortal and fallible and limited. It means that we are subject to illness and accident. It means that we cannot be everywhere at once; we cannot do everything that we would like to do; we are only able to do one thing at a time; we do and say things which are misunderstood; we often fail to appreciate what someone else is thinking. But the fact that we are spiritual means that we reach out towards immortality and freedom from limitations.

The real mystery of human life is the tension between, on the one hand, the limited nature of what we can do, the stumbling attempts at understanding ourselves and the world, the fact that there is always far more to do and to experience than we can possibly fit into our lives and, on the other hand, the unlimited, insatiable nature of our longings.

The human condition is a tension-in-unity between the eternal, which alone can satisfy us, and the passing moment, which is where we always find ourselves. We exist in tension between the material world and the spiritual values and insights that we find in it. But we cannot just escape into the spiritual sphere because it is only in the material world, through what we see and hear and feel, that we find the questions and the experiences and the relationships that point us to what is eternal. The human being finds the infinite in what is finite and limited. The life which God gives to us, is much more than mere existence in time. It is a drive towards fullness of life; *it is the seed of an existence which transcends the very limits of time.*[4]

That tension is the source of all great art and creativity. It is also where the spiritual dimension of our lives is understood. That is why the Church is the place where we ought to meet without any illusions, seeing ourselves more clearly,

- recognising that we are mortal, yet believing that we are called to the resurrection of the body and to the everlasting life which answers all our longings for immortality,

- recognising that we are fallible and sinful, but believing in the forgiveness of sins which answers all our longings to be healed and made whole,

- recognising our own inability to achieve justice and peace, our helplessness in protecting those we love from harm and from death, but believing that the Lord will wipe away every tear and make all things new.

I have often been struck by a passage from the French philosopher Gabriel Marcel. He was reflecting on the kind of thing that happens when two strangers meet at a bus stop or in a railway station. The may hold a polite conversation, perhaps about the weather. But there is a sense in which they do not really meet one another as their whole selves. They remain strangers; neither has any great interest in the other as a person:

> ... the strange thing is that the more the person I speak to is perceived as extrinsic to me, the more I am at the same time and in the same measure extrinsic to myself.[5]

To be members of the Christian Church is to try to see *one another* in the completeness of what we are, mortal yet immortal, material yet spiritual, vulnerable yet hoping for a fulfilment greater than anything we could construct or imagine for ourselves. That is what brings us to what the Pope was speaking of, the deep amazement that comes from seeing a person in the light of the incarnation and redemption.

One of the dangers in our culture is that there is a kind of eclipse of the sense of God which carries with it an eclipse of the sense of human dignity. Without an awareness of God, we fail to see ourselves as 'mysteriously different' and we risk beginning to regard the human person as,

> one more living being, as an organism which, at most, has reached a very high stage of perfection. Enclosed in the narrow horizon of physical nature, the human person is somehow reduced to being 'a thing', and no longer grasps the 'transcendent' character of human existence.[6]

The discussions that we hear from time to time about the possibility of creating artificial intelligence, about the creation of computers that would be more intelligent than any human being, seem to suggest that we are just complicated machines.

Of course, if you think that human beings are just machines, then there can be no reason in principle why it would not be possible to make machines which are more efficient. But human beings are not just machines. I do not believe for a moment that there will ever be a machine that could write genuine poetry, as distinct from well structured verse, or a machine that could paint a work of art, as distinct from an accurate representation or an elegant design, or a machine that could compose a musical masterpiece as distinct from a reasonably pleasant combination of notes.

Even if a machine could, by accident, produce something which would seem indistinguishable from a work of art, that would be nothing more than an accident – like monkeys typing Shakespeare. It would take a human being to recognise it as a work of art. A machine cannot be an artist because it can never feel the tensions between being limited in time yet longing for eternity, between knowing one's failures and hoping for forgiveness, between loneliness and the longing to belong.

A gift of God
But the most essential difference between human beings and machines, or between human beings and any other being on earth, was stated by Vatican II: 'Human beings are the only creatures on earth that God has wanted for their own sake'.[7] 'You are worth more than many sparrows' (Mt 10:31; Lk 12:7).

No other creature on earth can have personal relationships. No animal, however intelligent, can be another 'I'. However affectionate a dog may be, it cannot relate as one person to another.

That is the *third* point in Pope John Paul's list – to see human life as 'a life of relationship, a gift of God, the fruit and sign of his love'.

We are not simply able to relate to *one another*. More importantly, we are called to 'a life of relationship with God' which is 'the fruit and sign of his love'. Being a person is ultimately about the ability to relate to *God*. And the possibility of being related to God is something that God gives.

Many of the great philosophers of the past acknowledged the existence of God. What they did not dare to imagine was an intimate relationship in which we could address God as a loving Father who cares about us. That is possible because God first loves us:

> the invisible God, from the fullness of his love, addresses men and women as his friends, and lives among them, in order to invite and receive them into his own company.[8]

Sometimes people identify being a person with the actual ability to love and to speak. Then they begin to raise questions about whether a severely handicapped or comatose patient is really a person. If someone cannot relate to others, if they cannot express any seeking for truth and beauty, any longing for eternal life, how can they be regarded as a person? The way is thus opened for euthanasia and abortion.

The core of human dignity is not in anything that the person can do or achieve. It is in being a person who has been addressed by the Lord and who is invited into relationship with the eternal Father. To try to base human dignity on anything a person *does* or *possesses* rather than on what a person *is*, is to begin to undermine it.

It is also to miss the central point. The differences between people in terms of race and achievements and cultural inheritance may have a certain value and significance,

> But compared with the immeasurable values that go simply with being a [human being] – with being a spiritual creature loved by God, brother [or sister] to Christ, and with an unbreakable hold on eternity – these extra small ornaments, even if they have the values their possessors see in them, are almost comically insignificant.[9]

It is to begin to think that one person's fundamental rights are more important than another's:

> The criterion of personal dignity – which demands respect, generosity and service – is replaced by the criterion of efficiency, functionality and usefulness: others are considered not for what they 'are' but for what they 'have, do and produce'. This is the supremacy of the strong over the weak.[10]

The value of the human person lies in this, that from the first instant of a human life, there exists a being who is loved by God. Human life is a gift by which God shares something of himself.

> The divine origin of this spirit of life explains the perennial dissatisfaction which the human being feels throughout his or her life on earth ... Whoever heeds the deepest yearnings of the heart, must make their own the words of truth expressed by Saint Augustine, 'You have made us for yourself, O Lord, and our hearts are restless until they rest in you'.[11]

To each human being, however damaged physically or mentally, however undeveloped or however weak, the words of Isaiah can be applied: 'I have called you by your name, you are mine' (Is 43:1).

Even the least of these

The *fourth* characteristic of the Gospel of life is to proclaim that Jesus has a unique relationship with every person and that we can, therefore, see the face of Christ in every human face.

Everything that is good in each human being is already living in Christ. Because they are in him, they are passing through death into eternal glory. They are already part of the process of his death and resurrection. We will find again all the achievements, the solidarity, the creativity of this life in the eternal kingdom, as Vatican II put it, 'illuminated and transfigured'.[12]

That transfiguration points to a potential that is within all human goodness. Every time we recognise anything that is good in another person, we glimpse an aspect of the richness of our own destiny that we had not previously understood. People of every race, language, way of life, people of every temperament, of varied talents and characteristics – all will be at home with us and we will see how they are part of the glory of the Body of Christ to which we belong.

The more we recognise the face of Christ in another person, the more we appreciate the richness of Christ's Body. Each human being is a person whom we hope to welcome into the many mansions of our Father's house. More importantly, perhaps, each human person is someone who will, we hope, welcome *us*.

Each person is a facet of the whole glorious variety of God's giving of himself, the richness which is being gathered by and in Christ. To fail to see Christ in any human being is to fail to see some aspect of what we are called to be and what we are called to share – some aspect of our whole self.

I read an article recently in an Irish Sunday paper, written by a professed atheist. She was saying how contented she was in her atheism and how she had grown out of the guilt and superstition of her Catholic upbringing. She said that she tried to live with integrity and justice and compassion without seeing any need for 'the natural law'. Clearly she did not realise that the awareness deep in every human heart of the need to be honest and just and compassionate and so on is the natural law!

But she went on to say that a further element in her contentment is that she felt no need to forgive paedophiles or murderers or drug pushers. True enough, if one is an atheist, it is hard to see why one should be willing to forgive people who do such things. After all, when you reflect on it, no one ever has a right to be forgiven. You can never go to someone you have injured and say, 'I demand that you forgive me!' You can only ask them to forgive you. If the other person refuses, they are not denying you anything to which you are entitled.

Here, therefore, we come to a crucial difference. To see the face of Christ in every human face means that we do not simply see others as our equals, whose interests are no more or no less important than ours, so that we can, without qualms, look after our own interests and leave them to look after theirs. We see in them, rather, the one who forgives our sins, heals our wounds, draws us to his eternal life. 'Be generous to one another, sympathetic, forgiving each other as readily as God forgave you in Christ' (Eph 4:32). That is particularly true when we recall that he told us that the way we treat the least of his brothers and sisters is the way we are treating him.

Seeing the face of Christ in others means seeing in them the One whose mercy we have received. It means seeing that we have ourselves been forgiven. Like the man in the parable who had been forgiven an enormous debt, it makes no sense for us to be unforgiving to those who offend us (Mt 18:23-35).

The temptation to value people in terms of their usefulness or their achievements, whether actual or potential, is challenged by the Gospel. Again and again, the ordinary calculations are upended. It is the sinner who goes down from the temple justified, not the man who had done everything he ought to have done, and more. It was the poor widow with her pathetic coin who put most into the collection not the people who were throwing in large sums of money. It was the Man hanging helpless and in agony on the Cross who was changing the face of history and giving a new meaning to human existence.

There is no such thing as a human life which is no longer worthwhile. The judgment, as people express it when they are trying to justify euthanasia, that the quality of a person's life is insufficient, is a judgment that can hardly be made by someone who appreciates that the high point of human history and of the relationship between the human race and God was in the agonised, abandoned Man on the Cross.

It is one thing to recognise that there is nothing further than can be done for a person, that any further attempt at treatment will not be of benefit and is therefore not worthwhile. It is entirely another thing to decide that the person's life is not worthwhile and that it should be ended.

The gift of self

The highest form of the recognition of human dignity occurs when two people recognise in each other the face of Christ.

Implied in that recognition is the realisation that neither person should remain wrapped up in him or herself and that they are part of something greater than themselves. Self absorption is the enemy of human growth.

Human dignity is a bit like the word that you are trying desperately to remember. It comes to you only when you are not obsessed with it. It grows only in reaching beyond oneself to someone else.

To imagine one's own dignity as if one were alone in the universe would be a contradiction. That dignity, as we saw, is above all in the fact that God has related himself to us and that we are, therefore, brothers and sisters:

It follows then, that if human beings are the only creatures on earth that God has wanted for their own sake, they can fully discover their true selves only in sincere self-giving.[13]

Human dignity cannot be understood in an individualistic way. Sometimes it is imagined in that way – as if you could start with a person in splendid isolation and then begin to ask how he or she relates to others. The reality is that it is only through our relationship to others that we come to know ourselves at all. It is only because we need to communicate with others that we learn to speak. It is only by glimpsing ourselves as others see us that we come to understand ourselves and to escape from our illusions about ourselves. It is only by trying to respond to others that we discover and develop our own gifts.[14] We try to perfect ourselves not as some self-centred project, but in order to have a better self to give, a more whole self to give, to God and to others.

In that communication with others, we are not just expressing ideas and wishes and exchanging information. The way in which we relate to another person always expresses something of how we value them or, perhaps, devalue them and of how we value ourselves. Very often we can say, by our attitude, that things are more important than people or that the meaning of human life has to do with status or possessions or power. Alternatively, by giving ourselves, we can say that we are made for God, made for commitment, made for love.

That is why what was seen from the beginning as the supreme Christian witness, namely martyrdom, is also the supreme proclamation of human dignity. It is the clearest possible statement that the worth of a human being does not depend on anything we possess, not even on life itself, that it cannot be destroyed by anything that is done to us, even torture and perjury and injustice. It cannot be diminished by anything that is taken from us – reputation, liberty, the support of friends, even life itself.

Martyrdom shows that a human being is worth more than many sparrows. The human spirit doesn't have to be carried along by the strongest current or bow before a superior force.

That same dignity is shown in other ways. I often think that one of the most telling is the wedding promise. There, a man and woman, usually young, not knowing what the future may hold, commit themselves to one another, 'for better for worse, for richer for poorer, in sickness and in health'. They are saying, in other words, 'come what may, we will be true to each other'. They are saying, 'whatever life may throw at us, we will decide what we will be'.

Sometimes the future turns out to have much more of the worse, the poverty and the sickness. Nevertheless, in the majority of cases, couples live up to that apparently foolhardy promise. One of the greatest injuries which modern society does to young people is to suggest that the marriage promise is unrealistic, that all commitments are temporary and that relationships are necessarily unstable.

When the Pope describes the sincere gift of oneself as 'the fullest way to realise our personal freedom' he is pointing to the fundamental reason why we are worth more than many sparrows:

> For by their power to know themselves in the depth of their being [men and women] rise above the entire universe of mere objects. When they are drawn to think about their real selves they turn to those deep recesses of their being where God who probes the heart awaits them, and where they themselves decide their own destiny in the sight of God. So when they recognise in themselves a spiritual and immortal soul,

this is not an illusion, a product of their imagination, to be explained solely in terms of physical or social causes. On the contrary, they have grasped the profound truth of the matter.[15]

The human being decides his or her own destiny. That is something that sets us apart from every other creature on earth. Even the human being who dies as an infant, or whose brain is gravely damaged will one day do that, will respond in the deep recesses of their being to the God who approaches them and awaits them.

> The meaning of life is found in giving and receiving love, and in this light human sexuality and procreation reach their true and full significance. Love also gives meaning to suffering and death; despite the mystery that surrounds them, they can become saving events.[16]

The love that human life receives and gives is first of all the love of God. That is why, in order to appreciate who we really are, we need what the Pope calls a contemplative outlook which 'arises from faith in the God of life, who has created every individual as a "wonder"':

> It is time for all of us to adopt this outlook, and with deep religious awe to rediscover the ability to *revere and honour every person*...[17]

Notes
1. John Paul II, *Redemptor hominis*, 10.
2. John Paul II, *Evangelium vitae*, [EV] 2.
3. Rolheiser, R, *Irish Catholic/Catholic Herald*, 30 January 1997.
4. *EV*, 34.
5. G. Marcel, *Essai de Philosophie Concrète*, Gallimard, Paris, 1967, p. 55.

6. *EV*, 22.
7. Vatican II, *Gaudium et spes*, 24.
8. Vatican II, *Dei verbum*, 2.
9. F. J. Sheed, *Society and Sanity*, Sheed and Ward, London, 1953, p. 39.
10. *EV*, 23.
11. *EV*, 35.
12. *Gaudium et spes*, 39.
13. ibid., 24.
14. cf. *Gaudium et spes*, 25.
15. *Gaudium et spes*, 14.
16. *EV*, 81.
17. *EV*, 83.

THE HOLY SPIRIT AND THE MILLENNIUM[*]

The mother root

There is no lack of people to tell us that the Church is in a period of bleak winter, that the old Church is dying, that every statistic, whether it relates to practice, to belief or to vocations is pointing to decline. They can produce convincing evidence to back up that assertion. Of course, winter, and even death, should not necessarily be disastrous or even surprising for a Church that is founded on the triumph of the Cross and on belief in the life which is stronger than death.

There is, all the same, a lot that is painful about our situation. Perhaps the most important thing the pain does is to challenge us to reflect about the real source of life and hope. A poem by George Herbert, which is in the breviary, sums it up:

---

[*] An address delivered to priests of the Diocese of Cloyne, in Mallow on 21 November 1997.

> Who would have thought my shrivell'd heart
> Could have recovered greenness? It was gone
> Quite underground, as flowers depart
> To feed their mother root when they have blown:
> Where they together
> All the hard weather,
> Dead to the world, keep house unknown.

The appearance of death, which plants show in winter, is in fact a sign that renewal of life is taking place. The very worst thing that a gardener could do would be to dig frantically in an effort to restore what he imagined to be a dying plant. That would simply disturb the roots and disrupt the renewal which is taking place below the surface. There may be important work to be done on the surface during the winter, but panic is likely to be neither helpful nor appropriate!

In the document *Tertio millennio adveniente*, Pope John Paul expresses a serene confidence that this renewal of life is indeed happening. He says that what has been happening since the Second Vatican Council has 'made a significant contribution to the *preparation of that new springtime of Christian life* which will be revealed by the Great Jubilee, if Christians are docile to the action of the Holy Spirit'.[1]

It is no accident that he speaks about the action of the Holy Spirit. When the seed falls in good soil, the roots go deep; that is where the essential growth and strength come from. We need to think more than we do about the source of nourishment for our lives as Christians. We draw life from the Holy Spirit, the giver of life.

We have not been used to reflecting or speaking very much about the Holy Spirit. Yet the Spirit is at the heart of the life of the Church:

> United with the Spirit, the Church is supremely aware of the reality ... of what is deepest and most essential in

the human being, *because it is spiritual and incorruptible* ... This is human life in God, which ... can develop and flourish only by the Spirit's action. Therefore Saint Paul speaks to God on behalf of believers ... 'I bow my knees before the Father ... that he may grant you ... *to be strengthened with might through his Spirit in the inner man'.*[2]

No doubt in her deepest reality the Church is supremely aware of the action of the Holy Spirit which causes her life to flourish. But how aware are we of that action? You know the uneasy feeling one gets as, after the Our Father, the liturgy makes the contrast between our sins and the faith of the Church.

That passage from the encyclical on the Holy Spirit makes me suspect that, in a similar way, the Church's 'supreme awareness' of the Holy Spirit may often fail to be reflected in the awareness of most of us members of the Church! One of the primary tasks that the Pope sets before the Church is to develop *'a renewed appreciation of the presence and activity of the Spirit'.*[3]

It is an appreciation that is both more important and more difficult today than it was in the past. The life of the priest and of every Christian can be a strange combination of touching and celebrating great mysteries and rarely having the time, or perhaps never taking the time, to reflect on them. The kind of life that most people lead today, certainly the kind of life I lead, is one of feeling constantly on the verge of being overwhelmed, always falling behind, leaving half-done much of what I had hoped to do, torn between, on the one hand, trying to do six things at the one time and, on the other, the realisation that there are another sixty things I could usefully, maybe a lot more usefully, be doing but will never get around to.

It is one area where the life of the priest is, perhaps, more like that of lay people than either fully realises. Both of us are caught up in things that seem pressing and urgent, but that are ultimately trivial. At the same we are aware of more important issues that are being neglected.

Think for instance of all the endless variety of things that we feel guilty about. In his encyclical on the Mercy of God the Pope spoke about what he calls, 'the gigantic remorse caused by the fact that, side by side with wealthy and surfeited people and societies living in plenty and ruled by consumerism and pleasure, the same human family contains individuals and groups that are suffering from hunger. There are babies dying under their mothers' eyes'.[4]

And yet we know that, even if we spent twenty-four hours of every day trying to respond, there would still be an uncountable number of people who could not say to us, 'I was hungry and you gave me to eat.' It is good, therefore, to stop for a moment to reflect on the meaning of that phrase: the life 'which can develop and flourish only by the Spirit's action'.

It is not the running around and the increasingly frantic juggling of priorities and commitments that brings about a growth in the inner life or a sense of hope and meaning either in the people we serve or in ourselves. It is the Spirit's action that does that. And the Spirit's action is the life of the infinite God. In the face of the powerful life of the Spirit the signs of winter and of death are puny. We can and do feel helpless and discouraged, but nothing can conquer the love of God poured into human hearts; nothing is stronger than the Holy Spirit who is 'the eternal source of every gift that comes from God'.[5]

That is the foundation for our hope. 'We who have the first fruits of the Spirit, even we are groaning within ourselves as we wait for adoption as sons, and for our bodies to be set free. For in this hope we are saved' (Rom 8:23, 24).

The real reason for the feelings of discouragement and helplessness that are part of modern living is that we do not reflect enough on the truth, namely that beneath the surface of our lives and of the Church is the unconquerable life and the loving purpose of God: the life and love which are more powerful than death: 'If the Spirit of him who raised Jesus from the dead has his home in you; then he who raised Christ Jesus from the dead will give life to your own mortal bodies through his Spirit living in you' (Col 8:11). What Pope John Paul calls 'the desires of the Spirit' are 'exhortations echoing in the night of a new time of advent, at the end of which, 'everyone will see the salvation of God'.[6]

That all-powerful Holy Spirit is within us. The trouble is that all our rushing around may mean that we are never there within ourselves to meet him and to be strengthened. God is within us, Augustine says, 'but we are outside of ourselves' (*Confessions x*, 27).

He is at work particularly in our ministry as priests. We recognise that the Holy Spirit is at work in the celebration of the sacraments. We do not perhaps advert to the epiclesis where twice in each Eucharistic Prayer we invoke the Spirit so that the bread and wine may become the Body and Blood of Christ and so that we who share that Body and Blood may be brought together in unity.

We do not advert enough to the fact that in order that we could carry out the ministry of reconciliation, the first priests were given the Holy Spirit, the source of unity in the life of God and of communion with one another. 'Receive the Holy Spirit. If you forgive anyone's sins, they are forgiven' (Jn 20:23)

We believe that the life of God is growing in the person who receives the sacraments we celebrate, even when we feel less than enthusiastic, even when we feel we have not celebrated the liturgy well. But I suspect that we often lack that awareness, and that confidence, in the rest of our ministry and about the life of the Church in general. The Holy Spirit is at work, not only in the sacraments but 'in the variety of gifts and charisms, roles and ministries which he inspires for the good of the Church'.[7] We know that the powerful, unconquerable life of the Spirit is at work in many ways, and above all when people pray.

> It is a beautiful and salutary thought that, wherever people are praying in the world, there the Holy Spirit is, the living breath of prayer. It is a beautiful and salutary thought to recognise that, if prayer is offered throughout the world, in the past, in the present, in the future, equally widespread is the presence and action of the Holy Spirit who 'breathes' prayer in the human heart in all the endless range of the most varied situations and conditions, sometimes favourable, sometimes unfavourable to the spiritual and religious life.[8]

Problems of morale and problems of identity all come back to this mother root. We can begin to tackle those problems only if we understand how our lives are fed by the Holy Spirit. The question of who we are as followers of Christ can only be understood in the communion with him, and with all the sons and daughters of God, which is the work of the Holy Spirit. As priests, we are sent by the Father, in the person of Christ 'in order to live and work by the power of the Holy Spirit in the service of the Church and for the salvation of the world'.[9] Our identity, our morale, our confidence are based ultimately on this, that we work by the power of the Holy Spirit. That too is the basis of the identity and morale of the whole Church and of every Christian.

Renewing the face of the earth

The other side of that, of course, is that the Spirit's presence is not only comforting; it is also uncomfortable and challenging. The realisation that our ministry is founded on the all powerful action of God is consoling, but it cannot be a source of complacency; it is the very opposite. As Karl Rahner expressed it on one occasion:

> The Spirit of Pentecost is the spirit of holy unrest, of eternal discontent, the spirit that again and again startles us with the cry: 'You still have far to go', the spirit that makes even the saints dissatisfied with themselves ... the spirit that wills to renew the face of the earth, the spirit of life in ever new forms, on new roads, in new vehicles, on bold ventures.[10]

The converse of recognising that the life of the Church is the work of the Holy Spirit is the recognition that we are at the service of a goal that is greater and more surprising than we have imagined. The Holy Spirit, as we often pray without much thought, 'will renew the face of the earth'. That is a prayer that we would not say so easily if we stopped to ask ourselves what its fulfilment might involve.

What it means is that our most cherished plans and our fondest hopes are utterly inadequate, shallow, misguided and, literally, small-minded. What the Holy Spirit is bringing about is a universal communion in which every human being of every age and culture can feel fully at home. What the Holy Spirit is bringing about is a world without sin – no hatred, no cruelty, no dishonesty, no infidelity, no injustice. What the Holy Spirit is bringing about is a world without suffering – no death, no bereavement, no illness, no injury.

A little reflection on what that might mean, how different it will be from anything we imagine, is enough to give one a certain sympathy with Philip's question, 'Lord, we do not know where you are going, how can we know the way?' (Jn 14:5). The truth is that there is a sense in which Philip was absolutely right – we cannot know the way. Jesus is the way, but the precise paths along which the Spirit leads us to him are not clear to us. Our understanding of what the definitive Kingdom will be like is always through a glass darkly, but we need to be constantly reminded that it is infinitely bigger and more all-embracing than any plans we can formulate or imagine. Through reflecting on the Holy Spirit, Christians need to prepare for the millennium *'by renewing their hope in the definitive coming of the Kingdom of God'*.[11]

We can recognise the action of the Holy Spirit in the search for truth, wherever there are efforts for the promotion of justice, where there is opposition to violence and falsehood. That is relatively easy, but, as the French bishops put it some years ago:

> The Holy Spirit is never really received into our souls except when he disturbs our routine, sets our lives on fire and draws us on to greater courage and sharing in his work for the human race and for the gospel.[12]

It is one thing to make a fine sounding statement like that. But when we are faced with the fragility of human life and the failure of human ambitions, it is not so easy. The reality of it strikes when we are disillusioned by the failure of some undertaking in which we have invested a lot of ourselves and a lot of our hopes. Or when we are shattered by some loss that seems to undermine all we had hoped for. Or by some change in our health or our situation which means that nothing is going to work out as we had imagined.

The reality strikes when we walk along our road to Emmaus thinking, 'We had hoped that this plan or expectation or appointment or undertaking would have been the way that led to a growth of the kingdom of God'. And the response is the same one that was given to the first

Emmaus disciples: 'How foolish you are, and how slow of heart to believe all that the prophets have declared! Was it not necessary for the Christ to suffer these things before entering his glory' (Lk 24:25,26).

That is a lesson that each of us must learn as we walk the road with Jesus. The expansion of our horizons so that we can be stretched to receive the gift of God can be painful and shattering. And we are living in a world that is not comfortable with the thought of enduring pain, a world where we easily become aggrieved and easily see ourselves as victims. But the removal of things that had seemed essential to our well being is a necessary part of coming to know that our real destiny is so much beyond what we would have hoped for if left to ourselves.

The goal for which we work is not our kingdom but God's. The face of the earth is renewed according to his plan not ours – which is just as well! If any of us could renew the earth according to our plans, we might – though even that is unlikely – briefly satisfy ourselves. But the rest of the world's population would be less than thrilled to be asked to live in a paradise which we had designed for them! There is, on the other hand, never a good reason for disillusionment about the purposes of God or about the life of the Spirit.

The Spirit blows where he wills and as he wills, but that can be a hard lesson every time we have to learn it. Learning that lesson is the basis of the fruits of the Spirit, like joy, peace, patience. They are the fruit of knowing that this is God's world and God's church and that, unlikely as it may sometimes seem, God's Spirit is renewing the face of the earth.

Giver of gifts

Our hope is based on knowing that the all powerful Spirit is working in our world and in the Church. It is based, equally, on knowing that the Spirit is not just in what we are and in what we do but in all God's people. I sometimes catch myself at a Confirmation ceremony, waxing eloquent about the gifts of the Holy Spirit, about how great they are and about how they are given with such unlimited generosity. And I have to ask myself, do I act in practice like a person who believes that all those gifts are at work among the followers of Christ? I look at the parents, non-practising, living in irregular unions, in some cases quite hostile to the Church and all it stands for. Do I believe that in each of them the Spirit of God is present, leading them into the complete truth, or do I regard them as lost causes and take a perverse pleasure in the thought that they have to sit there and listen to me?

Do we actually expect to find the Spirit blowing where he wills – in the suggestions of that irritating parishioner? In the challenges of the media? In the complaints of women about how male dominated the Church seems to them? In the alienation of young people? In the ideas and initiatives of one's curate or parish priest, or even of one's bishop? The Spirit speaks in ways that seem to us to be most unsuitable and unlikely, considering that he has such an excellent instrument as ourselves available to him.

We might even ask ourselves whether we act like people who genuinely expect to hear the Spirit speaking in the magisterium of the Church or whether our first instinct is to join in the hue and cry about the latest 'controversial pronouncement'. I sometimes think that for many people, even good Catholics, their initial assumption is that papal encyclicals and documents should be presumed to be mistaken or at least that they should be treated with suspicion and scepticism until the contrary be demonstrated.

Awareness of the Spirit should give us a certain sense of expectancy, a reverence for the person who is the Spirit's temple, an openness to hear a new challenge, a readiness to receive an insight that can expand our understanding of what the Spirit is doing in our world. That openness to receive the activity of the Spirit is at the core of the Gospel. 'Faith, in its deepest essence', Pope John Paul said, 'is the openness of the human heart to the gift: *to God's self-communication in the Holy Spirit'.*[13]

That self-communication is made to each person, and it is made all the time. 'The Spirit makes present in the Church of every time and place the unique revelation brought by Christ to humanity, making it alive and active in the soul of each individual'.[14] Every priest has ample experience of the truth of what we say to the boys and girls at Confirmation about the greatness of the gifts of the Spirit and about how they are at work in each person making the revelation of God alive and active.

Openness to recognise that presence of the Holy Spirit is not just a new policy about lay participation. It is a theological imperative. If we believe that in Baptism and Confirmation the Holy Spirit is given with all those gifts and fruits, how dare we try to lead the Christian community without respecting that presence. That is putting it strongly, but not too strongly. We have no right to assume that the Spirit will speak in our parish or community only through us. He may be guiding the community by what the most unlikely parishioner is trying to say to us.

The community we serve is a community founded on the activity of the Holy Spirit. There are many different gifts, 'But at work in all these is one and the same Spirit, distributing them at will to each individual' (I Cor 12:11). The Holy Spirit makes us one body: 'The eye cannot say to the hand, "I have no need of you", nor can the head say to the feet, "I have no need of you".' (12:21). That warning applies first and foremost to us. We cannot say to any part of the body of Christ, 'I have no need of you'.

Indeed our ministry can only be sterile if it insists on trying to build a Christian community while not recognising the real life of the community 'which can develop and flourish only by the Spirit's action'. If we are not able, anxious, eager to recognise in others the gifts of the Spirit, gifts which the community needs and which we lack or do not possess to the same degree, then how do we expect to recognise and welcome Spirit in our own hearts. Whose work, then, are we doing?

The reality is that the communities we serve minister also to us. We are built up by the gifts of others as every Christian is. We know that the gifts of the Spirit are to be found in our parishes to a degree that is not our doing. There are examples of courage, and wisdom and reverence, there are instances of love and gentleness and patience, that far exceed anything in our own lives. They can humble us and challenge us. But they are above all, a strength for us. They show us the power of the Spirit on whom our own ministry depends.

All of that is easy to say, and we all know how to say the right things. We can talk about lay participation and collaborative ministry and the need for pastoral planning and consultation and renewal and the new evangelisation. There is a language of ecclesiastical correctness and we can all learn to speak it. But It does not take much reflection on our own experience of one another to know that the man who expresses the theory most eloquently is not always the most successful at putting it into practice!

The late Cardinal Tomás Ó Fiaich spoke about the lay members of the Church as a sleeping giant. He stressed how important it is that the giant should be awakened. He was, of course, absolutely right, but in our hearts we may be uncomfortably aware of the fact that giants are likely to break things and to create an awful lot of noise and confusion once they start to move around!

Being the Church

All of that is saying to us that the Holy Spirit is calling us to look at how we understand the Church. It is, perhaps one of the most crucial priorities for us today.

How far do we really see the Church as the sacramental reality in which

> Christ, who has gone away in his visible humanity, comes, is present and acts in his Church in such an intimate way as to make it his own Body. As such, the Church lives, works and grows 'to the close of the age'. All this happens through the power of the Holy Spirit.[15]

A phenomenon that is occurring in many parts of the world is a decline in organised religion paralleled by a huge increase in cults and superstitions and a more personal spiritual quest for meaning and alternative worldviews. That is the deepest reason why we have to look very carefully at the danger of allowing the organisational element in the Church to dominate the sacramental reality and the spirit of communion.

One of the great tragedies of the last few decades is that, in spite of the theology of the Church which we find in *Lumen gentium* of Vatican II, we have never had more talk about the structures and the politics of the life of the Church. The danger of focusing on the organisational aspect – even regarding it as a thing in itself, 'the institutional Church' – is that it suggests that the answer to that spiritual quest, that search for meaning, is not to be found in the Church.

This is partly related to the phenomenon of secularisation. Secularism does not necessarily deny religion, what it does is assign it a limited place. Religion becomes one of the things that people do – often 'tolerantly' regarded as a strange and eccentric thing – it is not seen as being about what people are. The institution is about what people do; the spirit is about what people are.

It is very necessary for us to keep our eye on the real meaning of being the Church. The reality is that, increasingly, it is the one context in which it is possible to recognise in any depth – and to celebrate – who and what we are.

One of the things that is worth reflecting on is that many priests complain of a sense of frustration and a sense of not being appreciated and affirmed. They feel like cogs in a machine that does not care about them. But we are not alone in that; it is a feeling that runs all through contemporary society.

One of the great sources of the anonymity that people complain of is that we do not meet one another as whole persons, we meet in our roles, as customers or clients or professionals or competitors. But that pushes us into living on the surface. The less we are fully involved with the other person, the less we are alive to ourselves.

The Church is a communion. That communion is the context in which we most fully face and answer the question, 'Who am I? Who are we?' Our relationship with God in the Holy Spirit enables us to understand our humanity in a new way, discover ourselves as belonging to Christ and as children of God, understand our dignity as 'the subject of God's approach and presence ... which contains the prospect and the very root of definitive glorification'.[16]

It is in the Church, when we gather to celebrate liturgy, that we acknowledge together our fallibility and mortality which focus the question of the meaning and destiny of human life. Is there any other context in which people gather proclaiming so openly that we are mortal, that we know this life is impermanent? Is there any other context in which we begin by announcing that we are all sinful and by confessing our sinfulness to God and to one another? Is there any other context in which we come realising that we are open to the infinity of God – to the eternal source of life and of the whole universe? Is there any other context in which we recognise that we are called to a commitment of all our heart and soul and might?

That is the great difference between communion and democracy – there is more to us than meets the state's eye. Democracy is a way of organising an aspect of our lives. It is a way of organising political society, organising us as citizens. That is why we can so easily accept the false assumption that the best democrat is the person without strong convictions, the person who does not rock the boat. It is a profoundly false assumption. It is the reason why democracy and all institutions, seem to be unable to generate real loyalty and enthusiasm: because one is expected to leave the real sources of that enthusiasm 'outside' as something private.

Isn't one of our problems that we have to some extent taken our eye off the truth of what religion is all about? Religion is about full personal involvement with others fully involved in recognising the truth about ourselves in the light of Gospel of Christ. 'The name for that deep amazement at human worth and dignity' Pope John Paul said, 'is the Gospel. It is also called Christianity'.[17]

It always strikes me that there is a profound difference between the image of the Church that one gets on a Sunday afternoon in Knock, and the image that emerges from the pens of some contemporary commentators. The first is an image of people wholeheartedly involved together; the second is of an institution being sneered at and attacked from the outside. The weapons of indignation and sarcasm are wielded by people who perceive themselves as outside that sense of common belonging. (Though the intensity of the feelings expressed may indicate that they are not as detached or as 'liberated' from it as they might wish to be.) There are many reasons for the tone of that criticism – personal hurts, a feeling of being rejected, resentment of a demanding, seemingly unreasonable, teaching which is seen as being delivered from an ivory tower and so on.

It is easy to empathise with some of that hurt. God knows we can often feel hurt and confused ourselves. But criticism made from outside that sense of belonging, that sense of touching the infinite truth together, misses the point. As Paul VI said somewhere about celibacy, if you are an agnostic then, from your point of view, it is absurd.

Why has this feeling of being outside the communion of the Church, of seeing it as an alien, unreasonable, limiting straitjacket, become so prevalent? To speak of the Church as our Holy Mother, like other hallowed phrases such as 'cherishing all the children of the nation equally' has instead become what one might call 'a hollowed phrase', emptied of its resonance. It seems that it can really only be spoken either reproachfully or sarcastically.

Part of the reason is that belonging to anything has become problematic. On the sports field we follow our teams wholeheartedly – though even there we may turn on the manager or even on a particular player. But any other loyalty – to country, to ideals, to individuals – tends to be seen as a kind of gullibility. Even commitments, like marriage, which are made sincerely and without condition, are increasingly fragile.

Part of the reason is that we have been shocked out of uncritical loyalty. We have seen the feet of clay in people and institutions that we had admired and trusted. But if we find ourselves having to look at every grouping to which we belong from some outside perspective and through suspicious eyes, then we will see first and foremost the structural aspects. We will see the parish buildings and parish accounts; we will see the ritual combat of the politicians; we will see the figures on marriage breakdown; we will see chains of command; we will see statistics about economic performance; we will see 'the institutional Church'. But if the end result is that we no longer feel a real sense of belonging to anything, then the baby has indeed been thrown out with the bath water.

In the end it is in the communion of the Holy Spirit that we are in touch with the questions and with the answer which is Jesus. In his encyclical *Evangelium vitae*, and indeed in the encyclical on the Holy Spirit, Pope John Paul paints a bleak picture of the culture of death – the arms race, poverty and famine, abortion, war and so on. We groan inwardly, says St Paul. 'Yes we groan,' the Pope adds, 'but in an expectation filled with unflagging hope, because it is precisely this human being that God has drawn near to, God who is Spirit'.[18]

One of the things we need to rediscover about the Church is that it is not first of all an institution. It is a community that is unique because it is founded by Jesus and he lives in it. It is unique because it is founded on knowing who we are – creatures of God, children of God. In the Church we face together the deepest questions about ourselves and our world – our fallibility, our mortality, the mystery of death, the longing for perfect peace and justice and happiness in a world where nothing is perfect or permanent. Facing our own humanity together should lead to a profound unity. It means hearing one another not so much on the level of issues and decisions but on the level of who we are. We are used to debating issues, to arguing points, but we need to learn a deeper kind of listening, where we hear one another's longing for the peace and joy of God.

I believe that something of that kind was at least part of the explanation for the amazing scenes at the funeral of Princess Diana. When did we ever before see thousands of people caught up in asking themselves about death and tragedy, and realising that no power or wealth or glamour or influence protects us from the inevitability of death? People are not used to facing these issues in a world that has often failed to leave them the space and the means to grieve at their own bereavements.

What the Spirit is saying
Another way of describing the challenge is that we are meant to listen to what the Holy Spirit is saying.

John, the author of the Book of Revelation, wrote short letters to the communities he knew – the Church in Ephesus, the church in Smyrna and so on (Rev 2:1-3:22). To each of them his parting words were: 'Let anyone who can hear, listen to what the Spirit is saying to the churches.' That might be our motto for the year ahead.

Most of the messages to the seven churches begin with a recognition of what is good in the life of the community: 'I know your activities, your love, your faith, your service, your perseverance, and I know you are still making progress.'

The messages then go on to point out how people's commitment is growing weaker. One famous passage says: 'Since you are neither hot nor cold, but only lukewarm, I will spit you out of my mouth.'

Finally the most important thing the Spirit is saying – a reminder of God's promise to those who hold on faithfully: 'Even if you have to die, keep faithful, and I will give you the crown of life for your prize.'

Our listening should follow the same threefold model:

- to recognise and give thanks for what is good, for the many gifts that exist among us, for the strong faith of so many people and the faith of those who went before us. In the first place, of course, this means giving thanks for the coming of Jesus Christ through the power of the Holy Spirit. 'What was accomplished by the Spirit's power 'in the fullness of time' can only through the Spirit's power now emerge from the memory of the Church'.[19] The memory of the Church also contains the heroism and the sanctity and the love of countless people down the centuries, not least in our own country. We need to hear and to recognise the Holy Spirit speaking in all of that history.

- to look at ourselves honestly in order to recognise where our faith has become half-hearted and how our parish and our diocese and the Church in Ireland could become a more vibrant community of faith. One of the characteristic activities of the Holy Spirit is to 'convince the world of sin'. He shows us the truth about sin in order to show us the truth about righteousness and justice.[20] That is, he enables us to see how sin is the source of suffering and distortion and blindness, how it conceals the truth about us. In doing that, he reveals himself and makes himself present in us 'as the Spirit of eternal life'.[21]

- to remind ourselves what the Holy Spirit promises to those who wholeheartedly love God and neighbour – the fulfilment of our deepest longings, the conquering of our greatest fears, the overcoming of every pain and injustice and sorrow. The virtue which is to be the focus of the Year of the Holy Spirit is the virtue of hope:

    > The basic attitude of hope, on the one hand encourages the Christian not to lose sight of the final goal which gives meaning and value to life, and on the other, offers solid and profound reasons for a daily commitment to transform reality in order to make it correspond to God's plan.[22]

That reminder of the presence and action of the Spirit is found in prayer:

> Prayer is ... the revelation of that abyss which is the human heart: a depth which comes from God and which only God can fill, precisely with the Holy Spirit.[23]

The call to prepare for the future is a call to the whole community of Christ's followers to help one another to *listen* so that we realise more clearly that the Gospel can transform our world just as much as it transformed the world of the apostles. In other words, the fruit of our listening will be a deeper conviction that the message of the Gospel is just as relevant in the third millennium as it ever was.

Another fruit of our listening will be to hear and recognise the gifts that are actually there in our communities. The whole exercise would be counterproductive if the first purpose of our listening were to try to see what somebody else should be doing. It is very important, I believe, that the first question to be asked by an individual, a group or a parish when it recognises a need is 'What can *we* do about it?'

It is not a matter of wondering whether somebody is going to produce a plan for the future of the Church in Ireland. It is a matter for each community and each individual to renew their belief that we have received the same powerful Gospel which sent the apostles out to change the world. We need to be ready to hear the Spirit repeating to us the message first written to the Church of Ephesus:

> I have this complaint to make: you have less love now than you used to. Think where you were before you

fell; repent and do as you used to do at first ... Let anyone who can hear listen to what the Spirit is saying to the churches: those who prove victorious I will feed from the tree of life set in God's paradise.

There is freedom

It is no accident that courage is one of the gifts of the Spirit. Renewing the face of the earth necessarily involves stepping into the unknown. There is something in all of us that would prefer to rest in what is familiar. It is too easy, 'to confuse the living endurance of the Church with the ossified habits in which we have established ourselves'.[24]

Tradition, the Pope said in his Apostolic Letter on the Eastern Catholic Churches (1995), 'is never pure nostalgia for things or forms past, nor regret for lost privileges, but the living memory of the Bride, kept eternally youthful by the Love that dwells within her' – in other words, by the Spirit.[25] Tradition needs to be balanced by expectation of the eternal kingdom – faithful to the events that gave birth to the Church, yet driven towards what we have not yet fully become. The whole of history is being gathered by the Spirit. The tradition and the expectation are one because they are both gathered into the eternal *now* of God. All that we do and experience is part of a life and a growth that develops and flourishes by the Spirit's action.

That is the perspective that gives us the courage, and therefore the freedom, to feel less alone, less as if everything depended on us, 'less enclosed in the narrow corner of our own individual achievement' or individual situation.[26] 'Where the Spirit of the Lord is, there is freedom' (2 Cor 3:17).

We are surrounded by fears – the fear of change, the fear of rejection, the fear of growing old and weary as we face an ever more demanding, hostile, unheeding world. There is the fear that the Church to which we have devoted our lives is in decline. There is the fear, shared especially with parents, that the future for Ireland is one in which Christian faith will not figure very largely. 'When the Son of Man comes', Jesus asked, 'will he find faith on earth?' (Lk 18:8) We find ourselves asking, 'When he comes, will he find faith in Ireland?'

These are all fears that would be utterly justified were it not for the power of God at work within us and within the baptised and confirmed people of God. That power of God, the Spirit of Christ is our strength. 'I can be proud,' St Paul says, 'in Christ Jesus, of what I have done for God. Of course I can dare to speak only of the things which Christ has done through me ... using what I have done, by the power of signs and wonders, by the power of the Spirit of God' (Rom 15:18,19).

Notes
1. Pope John Paul II, *Terto millennio adveniente*, 18.
2. Pope John Paul II, *Dominum et Vivificantem*, 58.
3. *Terto millennio adveniente*, 45.
4. Pope John Paul II, *Dives in misercordia*, 11.
5. *Dominum et Vivificantem*, 44.
6. *Dominum et Vivificantem*, 56.
7. *Terto millennio adveniente*, 45.
8. *Dominum et Vivificantem*, 65.
9. Pope John Paul II, *Pastores dabo vobis*, 12.
10. Karl Rahner, *Servants of the Lord*, Burns and Oates, 1986, pp. 123, 124.
11. *Terto millennio adveniente*, 46.
12. *Let us Proclaim the Mystery of Faith*, Veritas, 1979.
13. *Dominum et Vivificantem*, 51.
14. *Terto millennio adveniente*, 44.
15. *Dominum et Vivificantem*, 61.
16. ibid., 59.
17. Pope John Paul II, *Redemptor hominis*, 10.
18. *Dominum et Vivificantem*, 57.
19. ibid., 51.

20. ibid., Part II.
21. ibid., 48.
22. *Terto millennio adveniente*, 46.
23. *Dominum et Vivificantem*, 65.
24. Rahner, op. cit.
25. Pope John Paul II, *Orientale lumen*, 8.
26. ibid., 8.

The Soul of Europe[*]

The opening of the Irish Centre for Faith and Culture is the fulfilment of a hope expressed by Cardinal Paul Poupard when he visited Maynooth some years ago.[1] There are hundreds of such centres all over Europe: they are expressions of the search for what one might call the soul of Europe. 'We must never tire of saying and repeating to Europe: rediscover yourself! Rediscover your soul!'[2]

This of course involves the dialogue between faith and the growing non-belief of contemporary Europe. One of the most important things to recognise at the outset, however, is that the relationship between faith and culture is not the same as the relationship between belief and unbelief. The relationship between faith and culture exists within the believer him or herself. And without that inner dialogue, there will be no dialogue with the non-belief of others.

---

[*] An address delivered at the opening of the Irish Centre for Faith and Culture, St Patrick's College, Maynooth on 1 May 1997.

With both the cultural and the religious aspects of ourselves we face the question of what life means, what is its purpose. That is why we can hope that faith and culture can resonate with each other as, I trust, they will resonate in this Centre.

As the Celtic Tiger lopes majestically through the land, the uneasy question occurs to us, 'What is all this for?' We ask ourselves what we want our country to be. Is this the only ideal, we put before ourselves for our society – that it should be rich? When the inadequacy of that answer begins to dawn, then perhaps we are ready to hear again that we do not live on bread alone.

I am always a little puzzled when I see an advertisement for a course which is called 'Commercial French' or 'Commercial German'. I can't help wondering whether your average French industrialist is likely to be impressed by the fact that you know the French for 'Gross National Product', even though you may know nothing of French history or wine or music or literature. That may be unfair. I am sure that within a certain context an ability to use a technical vocabulary is very worthwhile. But it is a limited context; it is not the whole of human life or of human relationships. It may make possible a business negotiation, but not a meeting of minds and hearts! The example illustrates the point that if we operate on the basis that what one believes, what makes one tick, one's deepest feelings, are all private matters, then we could perhaps conduct public life in Commercial French or Commercial English. Worse still, maybe we already do!

A great deal of life seems to proceed on the assumption that one may safely ignore anything that may lie beneath the visible surface of things.

Nowadays there is a tendency to claim that agnosticism and sceptical relativism are the philosophy and the basic attitude which correspond to democratic forms of political life. Those who are convinced that they know the truth and firmly adhere to it are considered unreliable from a democratic point of view, since they do not accept that truth is determined by the majority.[3]

Of course, European history can scarcely allow us to forget the way in which the pursuit of deep convictions and loyalties can lead to conflict which destroys peace and social justice. But the answer to false and exaggerated convictions can only lie in the truth. It cannot be found in pretending that these convictions do not exist. If only the visible, functional aspect of ourselves is relevant to the public arena, then there is no need to seek further to find why our participation in the political process is less than wholehearted.

It is no accident that modern democracies, and the European Union itself, seem to be marked by a profound disillusionment with the political process. This is at least partly because the whole context risks seeming to tell people, 'Do not enter here with your whole self. Your religious views must be kept to yourself; they are a private matter. Your moral views must not intrude into political life, they are divisive.'

At the same time there is a certain rejoicing in the debunking of politicians and heroes, Churches and traditions, moral values and past achievements. One can, of course, only welcome the honesty which refuses to allow things to be swept beneath the carpet. But there is a danger that we may find ourselves with no heritage to be proud of and no foundation on which to stand. That would not only be dangerous, it would be an illusion. It might suggest that we are willing to delude ourselves that we are somehow better, more reliable, more honest, more enlightened, more virtuous than those who went before us. It might also suggest that we think ourselves capable of building a civilisation from scratch, that we have nothing to learn from our predecessors – or that we learn only from their failures not from their achievements. And so the contemporary atmosphere may be perceived as saying, 'Your loyalty to your nation, culture and beliefs is outdated and naïve. You have no past to be proud of; you are on your own.'

If we fail to think more deeply we risk building a society that is made up not of living people but of abstractions, with a life that is lived in the shallows by people without roots and without depth. We could end up with a society that forgets that its own foundations lie in a reverence for the dignity of the human person, in the kind of questions to which faith and culture respond each in its own way. What then is to stop us arriving at a society that believes only that what is profitable is good, what is legal is moral, what is bigger is better? A life based on such principles would necessarily be disillusioning.

Modern political societies get themselves involved in a kind of contradiction. They tend to regard religious beliefs and moral convictions as private matters to be respected from a safe distance but not to be allowed to interfere with public debate and decision making. Everybody seems to recognise that tolerance and pluralism are necessary. But pluralism cannot be based on the idea that the views and attitudes that are to be respected are mere matters of opinion which have no reference to the life of society. If you think my beliefs are just my idiosyncratic opinions and that I should not let them influence my vision of society, then you are not respecting them, because you are not recognising the significance which they have for me.

Each area of human understanding, scientific, historical, literary, sociological, philosophical or theological, reflects and advances our appreciation of what it means to be human; each expresses in its own way what it means to be human. 'Expressing what it means to be human' might not be a bad description of the role and meaning of culture! The dialogue between faith and culture is necessary for the health of both. A University is a meeting place for all of these areas of understanding. That is why it is so appropriate that this Centre should exist in this College to give rich expression to what it means to be human in the face of the uncertainties and fears and hopes of our times.

Faith and culture: mutual enrichment

The underlying fear in contemporary society is the fear of meaninglessness. We see a world in which people suffer and die in poverty and we do not want to send to ask for whom the bell tolls. We see the tragedy of young children killed in road accidents and fires and by cruel diseases and we are afraid to confront the question of how a world in which such things can happen can make any sense. We see the vast incomprehensibility of the universe and we have not the courage to ask whether we can still believe in a God who cares about puny and short-lived beings on this out of the way planet in an undistinguished galaxy. We are afraid of chaos.

If there is no meaning, then the search for truth is a mere illusion. The whole enterprise of culture becomes a nonsense. An oasis of meaning in an absurd universe would itself be absurd. Of course many philosophers and writers, for instance, feel themselves surrounded by chaos. At the same time, the very anguish which that evokes speaks of a commitment to the truth, a refusal to take refuge in evasions, which is closer than it might at first seem to the search for a truth which is permanently beyond our grasp.

Faith can be an ally of the cultural enterprise. It is a vision of meaning, of completeness, an assurance that there is an objective truth towards which the spirit can orient itself. It is an ally not an alternative. The Gospel does not terminate or replace the cultural quest because the meaning that is found in Christian faith is never fully grasped. There is interplay between poetic word and the Gospel message precisely because both are mysterious:

> If God's incomprehensibility does not ... draw us into his superluminous darkness, if it does not call us out of the little house of our homely, close-hugged truths into the strangeness of the night that is our real home, we have misunderstood, or failed to understand the words of Christianity. For they all speak of the unknown God, who only reveals himself to give himself as the abiding mystery ...[4]

The faith dimension of ourselves can only be the ally of the cultural on condition that we recognise the mysteriousness of what faith learns about God and about ourselves. If we adopt a complacent approach of 'faith has all the answers to what culture is seeking' then our faith would not only fail to be an ally of culture, it would fail to be genuine faith. Authentic faith has to be awe-struck, filled with wonder, humbling.

That is why it is equally true that culture can enrich faith. Faith can become empty if it is not stretched. The words of faith can lose their ability to touch the deepest chords. A few decades ago, phrases like 'sanctifying grace', 'incarnation', 'heaven' had a resonance that they seem to have lost. A few decades ago, the name 'Catholic Church' certainly had some negative overtones, but people were basically proud of the Church and had a sense of belonging to it. We believers need to renew the language of faith through its dialogue with culture so that the truths of the Gospel are spoken in a language that is nourished by, that illuminates and that challenges the culture in which it is spoken.

The process by which words become emptied of their meaning, by which 'hallowed phrases' become 'hollowed phrases' is not confined to the religious sphere. Only a few days ago an eminent member of the judiciary declared, as I understand it, that an abortion could appropriately be described as 'medical treatment'. Alas, poor Hippocrates!

The challenge that faces us is to hear the questions that are being expressed, in however halting and however inadequate and however hostile a manner in contemporary culture. We who are believers need to hear those questions not only from outside, but within ourselves.

We need also to help to pose the questions which our culture finds uncomfortable – questions about death and moral issues and the possibility of justice for the living and even for the dead. That is the task and the promise of the dialogue between faith and culture which will, I hope, be fruitfully conducted in this Centre which I am delighted and honoured to declare open.

Notes

1. Cardinal Paul Poupard, 'Creation, Culture and Faith', in *Cultures and Faith*, 1995 III-2, p. 93 Vatican City, also in *The Furrow*, May 1995, p. 280, 281.
2. John Paul II, to CCEE, 11 October 1997.
3. John Paul II, *Centesimus annus*, 46.
4. K. Rahner, *Theological Investigations 4*, Darton Longman & Todd, 1966, p. 359.

To the House of the Father*

No one has seen God

The Bible presents us with a God who is infinitely beyond human understanding. God was not to be represented by any image. He does not resemble anything in the universe. 'I am God, and there is no other; I am God, and there is no one like me' (Is 46:9).

Yahweh can only be approached with wonder, reverence and veneration. Moses was told to warn people that they should remain well clear of Mount Sinai when the Lord came down upon it: 'Take care not to go up the mountain or to touch the edge of it. Anyone who touches the mountain will be put to death' (Ex 19:12). No human being can look at God and survive. Even Moses himself is warned: 'You cannot see my face, for no one shall see me and live' (Ex 33:20).

We have nothing to offer which is not already his. 'With heaven my throne and earth my footstool, what house could

---

* First published as a pastoral letter, Advent 1998.

you build me, what place for me to rest, when all these things were made by me and all belong to me?' declares Yahweh. 'But my eyes are drawn to the person of humbled and contrite spirit, who trembles at my word' (Is 66: 1,2).

The dignity and the hope of the chosen people are based precisely on the fact that their God is infinitely beyond anything they could grasp or imagine: 'As the heavens are high above the earth, so great is his steadfast love toward those who fear him' (Ps 103:11).

We adore a God whom we cannot see and whose glory is beyond anything we know or understand.

The climate in which we live leaves little space for the reverence and the adoring silence by which one needs to approach to that inaccessible mystery of God. We deafen ourselves with noise and distraction rather than feel the emptiness in which the question of the meaning of life is heard.[1] We surround ourselves with striking and intense images rather than reflect on the immensity of the invisible God.

A sense of God's infinite mystery is central to any effort of renewal. It is fundamental to deepening our awareness of human dignity and invigorating our commitment to the mission of the Church in preparation for the Great Jubilee:

> There is no more urgent preparation for the performance of these tasks than this: to lead people to discover both their capacity to know the truth and their yearning for the ultimate and definitive meaning of life.[2]

But God who dwells in inaccessible light has made himself known in an entirely unanticipated way. 'No one has ever seen God. It is God the only Son, who is close to the Father's heart, who has made him known' (Jn 1:18).

The Father of Our Lord Jesus Christ

Jesus, born a member of our human family, knows the God of infinite splendour and power as his own Father. The Creator has revealed himself to us as the Father of our Lord Jesus Christ (Eph 1:3).

God's Fatherhood is altogether unique. A human father becomes a father at some stage during his life. Fatherhood is an aspect, however important, of the whole person who also has other experiences and commitments and relationships. Human fatherhood cannot exist without motherhood. Being a human parent is a shared reality.

In God none of these considerations apply. God does not become Father, but is Father from all eternity. Fatherhood is not an aspect of his person; it is his Personhood. With all his infinite Being, God the Father begets the Son. Fathering is not something he does, it is *who he is*.

God the Father is the sole origin of the Son. God's Fatherhood, the begetting of the Son, is neither feminine nor masculine.[3] It transcends any human parenting. It is as much the source and model of motherhood as it is of fatherhood. The seventh century Council of Toledo speaks of the Son being 'generated or born *from the Father's womb*'.[4]

So, 'each of the two sexes is an image of the power and tenderness of God, with equal dignity though in a different way'.[5] 'God's parental tenderness can also be expressed by the image of motherhood, which emphasises God's immanence, the intimacy between Creator and creature'.[6]

The intimacy of the relationship between Jesus and his Father is utterly new. He addresses God by a name, *Abba*, which is used only by sons and daughters within the family. It means something like 'Dad'. Nobody would have dreamt of using so familiar a word in speaking to the Creator of the universe.

But Jesus said to his followers, 'When you pray, this is what to say: Father' (Lk 11:2). We too are to call God *'Abba'* (Rom

8:15). 'To all who received him, who believed in his name, [Jesus] gave power to become children of God' (Jn 1:12).

God is the Father of a human being, our Brother. He is the Father of a Man who died the most barbaric and unjust death. In offering his whole life, his whole self, to his Father on the Cross, Jesus, the perfect Image of his Father, shows what God is like.

First of all he shows that God's love is extravagantly merciful, beyond all expectation, given to those who in no way deserve it: 'God proves his love for us in that while we still were sinners Christ died for us' (Rom 5:8).

Secondly, he shows that the love of God is more powerful than anything we fear. The Father accepts the self-offering of Jesus and receives his human body into the glory which belongs to the Son before the world was made (Jn 17:5). In his resurrection, the Son receives the love of the Father which is more powerful than death and more powerful than evil.[7] We too are promised a new creation where death and mourning and crying and pain will be no more (Rev 21:4). There will be no more night and the Lord God will be our light (Rev 22:5).

Making the Father known

Jesus tells us about his Father – and ours. The Son, who is close to the Father's heart, makes him known.

His own Father was, no doubt, very much in his mind when he told the story of the two sons whose father loved them deeply (Lk 15:11-32). It is worth reflecting on the three characters in that parable which we call 'the prodigal son'.[8]

When the first son, an impatient young man, demanded everything that was due to him and set off to make his fortune, the father did not stand in his way. He made no attempt to force him to stay.

When things went disastrously wrong, the young man decided to swallow his pride and go home to his father's house. It was remembering his father that prompted him to realise that it would be possible to return. It was the father's love which drew him home, more gently but more powerfully than if an army had been sent to compel him.

On his return, the welcome he received was far beyond anything he had imagined. It is, as someone once remarked, 'the story of a father's jubilant forgiveness'. The father was not just hoping for his return; he was running out to meet him. The son hoped that he might be allowed to live in his father's house as a servant. Instead he was dressed in the best robe and a ring was placed on his finger, marking his restoration as a son of the household. A feast was organised because, 'this son of mine was dead and has come back to life; he was lost and is found'.

The second son, a much less adventurous type, was not a bit pleased at this turn of events. Nobody had ever made that kind of fuss about him, even though, unlike his brother, he had lived a blameless life. He was angry and refused to go in.

Again the father left his house and went out, this time to find the elder brother. He wanted to assure him that he too was loved: 'You are with me always and all I have is yours. But it was only right that we should celebrate'.

When he saw the younger son returning, bruised and humiliated by his experiences, the father was 'filled with compassion'. When he saw that the elder brother was aggrieved, he was anxious to bring him also into the family celebration. That was his fundamental attitude towards both of his sons.

Unconditional love
Whatever his sons did, the attitude of the father in the parable remained unshakeable – he was their father. That is what God is like. The Father of our Lord Jesus Christ describes himself as, 'God of tenderness and compassion,

slow to anger, rich in faithful love and constancy' (Ex 34:6).

Even when people are called, like the prodigal son, to make painful, humiliating, and perhaps lengthy, journeys back, God continues to offer a welcome: 'I will punish their offences with the rod ... but I will never take back my love' (Ps 89:33).

God is utterly reliable and untiringly faithful. His words and promises will be fulfilled (Num 23:19). He remains unshakeably the Father. He does not change (Mal 3:6); in spite of anything people do, he is willing to receive them.

That is why the Year of the Father is also the year of the sacrament of Penance, the sacrament of the Father's ready welcome and jubilant forgiveness. There is joy in heaven over one sinner who repents (Lk 15:7) because one of the Father's children was dead and is alive again, was lost and is found.

But the sacrament of Penance or Reconciliation cannot be understood simply in terms of the ceremony which takes place in the church or at a sickbed.

A sign of reconciliation

Our whole life as a believing community is meant to be, as it were, a sacrament of reconciliation – a sign and an instrument of the merciful love of God in the world.[9] That is true first of all because of what the Church is – a community of people who believe and hope in the mercy of God and who are called to continue Christ's work and to proclaim his Good News.

The Year of the Father is an invitation to everyone to come home to the Father. It is an invitation to realise that coming home to our Father is what Christian living is all about:

> The whole of the Christian life is like a great pilgrimage to the house of the Father, whose

unconditional love for every human creature, and in particular for the 'prodigal son', we discover anew every day.[10]

That invitation is not issued simply from pulpits and through pastoral letters. Those who approach the sacrament of Penance are forgiven by God. They are at the same time restored to the family of the Church which works for their restoration 'by charity, by example and by prayer'.[11]

The Year of the Father is a time for renewing our efforts to be the kind of community which, like the father of the prodigal, goes out to meet those who need to know that they are welcome. Do people who have drifted away from a sense of belonging to the Church, or people whose lives have led them into situations out of harmony with the values to which the Church tries to witness, or people involved in disputes and tensions between themselves, or people who are strangers among us, see in us a love which is welcoming, unshakeable, longing to forgive, to reconcile, to unite?

Do young people looking for full participation in the life of the parish and of society, people who are bereaved, people for whom the moral teaching of the Church is a particular challenge, people who have a difficult economic struggle, or who have their own crises to meet in their family life, find in their parish, 'a fraternal and welcoming family home, where those who have been baptised and confirmed become aware of forming the People of God'?[12]

These are some of the questions that we have been putting to ourselves during the Listening Process. In the coming year, as we try to respond to some of these needs, it will be important to remember the awesome meaning of what we are trying to do. We are trying to be what God has called us to be. The God who made himself known as a mysterious presence on Mount Sinai and in the Holy of Holies in the Jerusalem Temple, the God who revealed himself in his only Son made flesh, is now present in the Church. Jesus comes with his Father to make their home in each one who accepts him (Jn 14:23).

It is our task, in the coming year, to try to make more visible the Father's love present within us. It should be possible to see reflected in us the power, the tenderness, the welcome, the jubilant forgiveness of the Father of mercy.

Freedom and slavery
To find ourselves in the parable, we need to look more closely at the two brothers. The story is really about the failure of either of them to understand his father. Both had failed to grasp how all embracing and unconditional his love was.

The younger man saw life in his father's house as a restricting thing. 'If I could be free of it,' he thought, 'I could build my own life the way I would like to have it'. But the kind of life he envisaged was unrealistic and illusory. 'He squandered his money on a life of debauchery'. Very quickly, of course, the money was gone, along with the friends he thought he had made.

Sometimes a situation can seem limiting. What is certain, however, is that it is even more frustrating to try to live an illusion. That is what Dorothy Parker called 'the flaw in paganism':

> Drink and dance and laugh and lie,
> Love, the reeling midnight through,
> For tomorrow we shall die!
> (But, alas, we never do.)

We may try to live without a thought for the meaning or the consequences of our actions, but there is a meaning, and there are repercussions – not least on ourselves – beyond the immediate moment.

Thus it sometimes happens that, when we think we are freeing ourselves we are actually becoming trapped – by possessions, by setting out on a path that is lacking in integrity, by deceit, by ambition. What starts out looking like freedom can end up looking like slavery.

More importantly, the young man saw life at home as restricting precisely because he did not understand his father's love. His life became a burden because it was merely a duty.

The same thing can happen our approach to Christian living:

> Those who live 'by the flesh' experience God's law as a burden, and indeed as a denial or at least a restriction of their own freedom. On the other hand, those who are impelled by love and 'walk by the Spirit' (Gal 5:16), and who desire to serve others, find in God's Law the fundamental and necessary way in which to practise love as something freely chosen and freely lived out.[13]

For the prodigal son, his relationship with his father was a burden, an arrangement. He began by demanding that the value of his inheritance should be calculated in terms of 'the share of the estate that will come to me'. It was as if his relationship to his father was an economic asset that could be cashed in.

After all his disastrous experiences he began to come to his senses. He recognised that he had to set out on a return journey, a pilgrimage to the house of the Father. But still he did not understand the father's unconditional love. He returned thinking in terms of a calculation, or a negotiation: 'treat me like one of your hired hands.'

The father would have none of it. The son was not even allowed to make the proposal. The issue was not what the son had done or what he deserved. *Nothing the son could do would alter who his father was.* Whatever had happened he remained a father and therefore the young man had never ceased to be a son.

The bargaining and the calculations completely missed the point. This was not about what was owned or earned or owed. It was about a relationship that the father could never abandon or deny. This year is a time when the Church is called to try to proclaim the Father's unchangingly welcoming love.

I hope that, in this pastoral letter and in the life of the parish and diocese, you may hear the echo of a personal call from the Father whose love for you never wavers.

Fathering is not something God does, it is who he is. God never abandons or denies anyone. God's love draws everybody, including those of whom we are tempted to despair, or those of whom we most strongly disapprove, to his home. There we hope to join them.

I have never disobeyed
That thought would have been too much for the elder brother. For him, it was clear that there were some people, like his irresponsible younger brother, who had put themselves beyond the reach of forgiveness.

He had no sense that he had a journey to make. There he was in his father's house. It was something he took for granted. It was something he had earned: 'All these years I have slaved for you and never once disobeyed any order of yours'.

He too was thinking in terms of a bargain or an arrangement. His life was a burden for which he deserved payment. He deserved the fatted calf more than someone who had so obviously disgraced himself.

He missed the point every bit as comprehensively as his brother. His work record would, perhaps, have made him a reliable hired hand. *It was not what made him a son.*

The father's love for both was unconditional. He loved them because he was their father. Each of them had to make a journey, a pilgrimage, in order to discover that unconditional love anew. We are sons and daughters of God because he is our Father, not because of how good our behaviour has been. Everything – our freedom, our talents, our ability to do anything at all – is his gift. Nothing we do can impress the God who created all we have and are and know! We can do nothing to place God in our debt. Rather we are meant to discover anew each day the unconditional love of the Father for every human creature.

That is why it misses the point to say, as one sometimes hears said, 'If you are just and kind and honest, that's the main thing; that's what being a Christian is all about'. Being a Christian is first of all about knowing that we are on a pilgrimage to the house of our Father who loves us unconditionally. It is about knowing that we can call God 'Abba' because we share in the relationship of Jesus Christ, God's only Son, to his eternal Father. It is about knowing that we can call God 'Abba' because the Spirit of God has been poured into our hearts (Rom 8:14-17).

The elder son, for all his conscientious, virtuous behaviour, depends on his father's generosity every bit as much as the younger son. The father's extravagantly generous love is a reproach to both of them. That is the lesson of the parable.

'And' not 'But'

We are tempted, in speaking of God's unconditional love, to introduce a 'but'. 'God loves you, *but* you have to repent. God loves you *but* you have to keep the commandments.' The 'but' seems to suggest that if we sin, God will no longer love us. That is what the elder brother in us thinks: 'Surely the father's love cannot extend to somebody who has acted so selfishly and so irresponsibly!' That too is what the younger brother in us thinks. 'My father will never treat me as he used to do before I made such a mess of my life'.

The lesson of the parable is that it is the sinner who changes, not God. The Father of our Lord Jesus Christ is Father with his whole unchangeable Being. Nothing that a creature does or fails to do can change who He is. God's unwavering love calls us to make a pilgrimage to the house of the Father.

From the first realisation that he could return, through the journey home, the jubilantly forgiving welcome and, no doubt, in the years that lay ahead, the younger son grew in understanding of his father. Life at home was now no longer a burden but a loving, unselfish, loyal response which tried to reflect the lavishly unlimited love he had received.

After the shock of seeing a love which had no 'buts', a love which never falters, perhaps the elder brother too entered on a journey of growth in understanding of his father. Perhaps he too came to a response motivated not by calculation and self-interest but by a sense of loving gratitude. Perhaps he began to learn that what he had received was not a payment he had earned but a gift which he had not, and could never have, deserved.

There is no limit to the demands which the unconditional love of God makes on us. We are to love him with all our heart and all our soul and all our strength (Dt 6:5). We are to love one another as Jesus loves us (Jn 13:34), in other words just as the Father loves him (Jn 15:9). There is no higher standard and all of us fall infinitely short of it.

The relationship of God's love to the way we should live is not a 'but'; it is an 'and therefore'. God loves us unconditionally *and therefore*, like the prodigal son, we are called to change the way we live; we must arise and go to the Father who welcomes us. God loves us unconditionally *and therefore*, like the elder brother, we ought to rejoice at the generosity of that love even, or rather *especially*, when it is lavished on those whom we regard with disapproval.

God loves us unconditionally *and therefore* we must be ready to forgive even those who most grievously hurt us. God loves us unconditionally *and therefore* we must refrain from exploiting or deceiving or defrauding, or despising, or abandoning any of the sons and daughters whom he loves. God loves us unconditionally *and therefore* we must be ready to forgive as generously as he is willing to forgive us (Lk 11:3,4, Mt 18:23-35).

That love reproaches us, challenges us, judges us, not because the Father has turned his back on us, but because he would never turn his back on us. We have fallen short of the love of a Father who longs to welcome our return:

> When we realise that God's love for us does not cease in the face of our sin or recoil before our offences, but becomes even more attentive and generous; when we realise that this love went so far as to cause the Passion and Death of the Word made flesh who consented to redeem us at the price of his own blood, then we exclaim in gratitude: 'Yes, the Lord is rich in mercy', and even: 'The Lord is mercy'.[14]

God is love

The coming year will bring us to the threshold of the third millennium. It is a year for reflecting on the most profound and most awesome truth: 'God is love' (I Jn 4:8,16).

The whole being of the Father is his giving of his entire self to the Son. That act of self-giving, that Fathering, is who he is. The entire life of the Trinity is an unlimited flow in which the infinite nature of God is given and received without any holding back. The same divine nature belongs totally to Father, Son and Holy Spirit. The fundamental message of the Gospel is that we have been made sons and daughters of God. 'The Spirit himself joins with our spirit to bear witness that we are children of God ... heirs of God and joint heirs with Christ, provided that we share his suffering so as to share his glory' (Rom 8:16,17).

We live in a world which is uncomfortable with silence and solitude. We often feel caught in frenetic activity, we are perpetually busy. But we are not good at asking what it is all for. It is a world which is interested in everything about the life of the Church except the question of whether that fundamental message is true and the question of what the implications of that truth might be.

We are meant to be a sign in the world of that truth. That is why we are called to love our neighbour – not so that we can impress God but so that we can share the love we have received.

Our first task is to learn the lessons that the two brothers were taught, the lesson that our Father's love is infinitely greater than we know. That is where our pilgrimage to the house of our Father begins. That is the first step in living out the vocation and mission that the Father has entrusted to us:

> This pilgrimage (to the house of the Father) takes place in the heart of each person, extends to the believing community and then reaches the whole of humanity.[15]

Go gcoinní Rí na glóire ar bhóthar ár leasa sinn.

Notes
1. cf. John Paul II, *Orientale lumen*, 16.
2. John Paul II, *Fides et ratio*, 102.
3. cf. John Paul II, *Mulieris dignitatem*, 8, *Catechism of the Catholic Church* (CCC), 239.
4. DS, (1966), 526.
5. CCC, 2335, cf. 369.

6. *CCC*, 239.
7. John Paul II, *Dives in misericordia*, 8.
8. cf. John Paul II, *Reconciliatio et paenitentia*, (RP), 5,6.
9. *RP*, 11.
10. John Paul II, *Tertio millennio adveniente*, (TMA), 49.
11. Vatican II, *Lumen gentium*, 11.
12. John Paul II, *Catechesi tradendae*, 67.
13. John Paul II, *Veritatis splendor*, 18.
14. *RP*, 22.
15. *TMA*, 49.

OUR COMMON VISION OF HUMANITY*

The dying months of the nineteen hundreds saw a very important step, namely the signing of the Joint Declaration on the Doctrine of Justification between the Catholic Church and the World Lutheran Federation on October 31st. The Declaration stated that: 'The understanding of the doctrine of justification set forth in this Declaration shows that a consensus exists between Lutherans and Catholics.' Please God this will prove to have been a prophetic way of bidding farewell to the millennium of Christian divisions, pointing, before the new century has advanced very far, to further substantial steps on the road to the unity for which Christ prayed, so that the world might believe.

Unity does not mean that we will all simply become the same and that everything which is different about us will simply disappear. Some of the differences that exist

---

* First published in *Doctrine & Life* as 'Is Ecumenical Consensus Possible on Moral Questions', also delivered at the Ecumenical Day for the Clergy, Kylemore Abbey, 24 January 2000.

between our various traditions are part of the abundant variety of Christian history, life and worship. They are gifts by which we can enrich one another. These are not differences to be overcome but differences to be appreciated and celebrated.

Even some of the more negative elements of our history have a positive aspect. The Joint Declaration states that the doctrinal condemnations issued by each side in the sixteenth century do not apply to contemporary Lutheran and Catholic doctrine as set out in the Declaration. But it goes on to say that these condemnations should not be seen in a totally negative light. The document says: 'Nothing is thereby taken away from the seriousness of the condemnations related to the doctrine of justification. Some were not simply pointless. They remain for us "salutary warnings" to which we must attend in our teaching and practice'.[1] In other words, the people who were divided at the time of the Reformation were, on both 'sides', defending important perspectives on the truth and we can learn from each other what it is that our traditions were so anxious to defend.

There are, however, aspects of our divisions in which we cannot rejoice. The greatest of these is, as Cardinal Cassidy pointed in a reflection on the Joint Declaration which he signed on behalf of the Catholic Church, '... we do not yet share the "oneness in faith, worship and ecclesial life" which, for Catholics, is required for Eucharistic sharing. Our common participation in the Eucharist awaits the full ecclesial communion which we seek, and for which the Eucharist will be the sign par excellence'.[2]

What I would like to reflect on today is another area of division between us which does not receive the attention it deserves. A great deal of ecumenical effort has been expended in relation to those theological and ecclesiological issues which have divided us since the Reformation. But there is another area we need to look at. In Ireland as elsewhere, the Churches are often seen to speak with divided voices on socio-moral issues. I'm thinking of the whole area of bio-ethics, or questions about how far and in what way moral considerations should influence legislation. It is surprising how rarely we seem to discuss these differences in any serious way. It seems obvious that we need to identify their source and to place them in the context of our fundamental unity as disciples of Christ who is the Way.

One of the few efforts to do this was the important ARCIC Statement, *Life in Christ, Morals, Communion and the Church*, published in 1994.

I believe that this reflection is very important. We are in the middle of an upheaval in terms of moral values. New questions are piling in on us – research into the human genome will raise fundamental issues that we have never faced before. Extraordinary advances in health care pose questions about the rational use and the just distribution of medical resources. The question of whether the damage we are doing to our environment is an irreparable act of irresponsibility is becoming increasingly pressing. The rhetoric about human rights which marked the last half of the twentieth century is crying out for implementation in respect of even the most elementary fairness in providing for the life, health care, education and housing of people in the developing world. The question of what kind of values can underlie and sustain the unity of a pluralist society urgently needs to be addressed.

At the same time, there are constant complaints, some of which are directed at us, the ordained ministers, about a certain lack of vision, inspiration and leadership. There are all sorts of reasons for that, not least the scandals that have been revealed in Church and State. People have become less inclined to trust anyone who seems to be claiming the high moral ground. It sometimes seems that they are demanding, quite unreasonably, that nobody should express a moral principle unless they have always perfectly observed it themselves. This can be uncomfortable for us who have a responsibility to preach the Gospel in its implications for how we live as well as in its implications for what we believe.

But there is, I suspect, another, even more fundamental explanation for this sense of being rudderless. Part of the reason why people no longer look to the Churches for direction in the way they used to is that they have come to think that it is not possible to have a common moral vision which can guide the complex form of society that has now emerged. In some respects morality, like religion, is seen as a private matter – even though there are issues such as ecology, food safety, and integrity in public life for instance, which are seen as public concerns in a way that was not the case in the past. But in many other areas of moral concern – even when there are clear public implications – people feel surrounded by a whole series of competing moral visions. They are also aware that a morally and culturally and religiously plural society cannot function unless we are all pluralist and tolerant in our outlook.

But the net result can often be that people conclude that there is no such thing as moral truth. If someone claims that they are acting according to their convictions, following their conscience, we recognise that this position is worthy of the greatest respect. We tend to go further and to act as if each person's conviction, each of the wide variety of moral opinions that we encounter, could be equally true.

I am convinced that a great deal of the lack of direction in our social life, a great deal of the apparent lack of leadership, arises from the fear that there is not and cannot be any coherent moral framework in our kind of society. How can we have leadership if we do not know how to come to any agreement about where it is we wish our society to go?

The reason why it is important for us to reflect on our differences in the moral area, just as much as in the area of ecclesiology, is that it is surely the role of the Churches to present a moral vision that will be convincing and transforming.

And we do have such a vision. We are proclaimers of the Good News about the meaning of human life in the light of the Incarnation and Redemption. We have a vision which should be able to express what Pope John Paul called 'deep amazement at human worth and dignity' in the light of the Incarnation and Redemption. How precious human beings must be 'if God "gave his only Son" in order that [we] "should not perish by having eternal life"'.[3] We should have something to say about living a life worthy of the vocation to which we have been called (Eph 4:1).

That vision is what most fundamentally underlies the Christian challenge to the various illusions and distortions which blight and cheapen our social life: the *greed* that sets out to take care of one's own interests, whatever the cost to one's integrity or to the well being of others; the *materialism* that values a person more for what they earn than for who they are; the *conformism*, often passing for liberalism, which fails to see any need for a fundamental critique of the values that surround us but contents itself with decrying the perceived blindness of the past; the *permissiveness* that can demean human sexuality and all human relationships and which often demeans women in particular; the *lack of reflection* that tends to blot out any sense of the transcendent God and allows people to live by empty and unsatisfying slogans – at least until a crisis strikes. In all of these areas, and in others, we have a vital challenge to make.

Perhaps challenge is the most appropriate word. It is not a question of the Christian Churches trying to dictate answers. We do not have, nor would we wish to have, the power to dictate. Situations in history where Churches did exercise coercive power never did much to advance real Christianity. The only influence that we can have on attitudes is by appealing to the consciences of individuals. That influence can be a strong one – and there is no reason why we should apologise if Christian values strongly influence people's attitudes. If the message fails to make sense to them, they will, presumably, ignore it. There is nothing we can do about that except to wonder whether we have fallen short in our manner of communicating the Gospel.

But we are obliged to try to communicate the vision. It would be naïve to think that, if the Churches failed to speak, people would be 'left to make up their own minds'. The efforts we make to influence people's attitudes will never be more than one small voice in the cacophony that surrounds everybody today.

We cannot dictate. Neither can we pretend to economic and political expertise, which Churches as such simply do not possess. Our role is to ask people, and to help people, to reflect on the reality of human dignity, and especially to ask Christians to reflect in the light of the Gospel, and to try to put the implications of that reflection into practice. In other words we should be reflecting and asking people to reflect about how in practice we can love one another as Jesus loved us.

The fact is that we do a great deal of that, often, thank God, together. When it comes to the challenges of violence and poverty and the demands of integrity, the Churches frequently do speak unanimously and, often enough, quite eloquently. It is all too obvious, however, from criticisms one hears even from within the Churches that such voices are easily lost or forgotten. We are frequently accused of 'saying nothing' about issues which have been repeatedly addressed. Our consensus on so many issues and the difficulty of being heard are all the more reason why the unravelling of this Christian consensus in other areas deserves more attention than we usually give it.

In his document following the Synod of Bishops in 1983, the Pope spoke, rather startlingly, about a 'real overthrowing and downfall of moral values'. He went on to say: 'the problem is not so much one of ignorance of Christian ethics but ignorance rather of the meaning, foundation and criteria of the moral attitude'.[4] He was concerned not so much with particular moral issues as with the way that we do our moral thinking.

That is a fundamental area that we need to explore together. One has only to read or to hear moral discussions on controversial issues to recognise that they are often going nowhere.

One fundamental reason for that is a philosophical one. What is really happening in many of these arguments is not so much a theological division as a philosophical one. Different theories of moral analysis are working, often unrecognised. A number of strands are often mixed up in people's minds. If one tries to unravel them one oversimplifies, but one might detect some of the following approaches.

To a certain extent people are operating on the basis of how they feel. Moral attitudes are seen as a kind of intuition. It is not really possible to explain that feeling or instinct to a person who does not share it. This works well enough in some instances, and I suppose, in practice, it is how many of us actually respond to various issues. We all feel revolted by slavery and torture and exploitation of those who are less fortunate than oneself. This reflects a quite respectable philosophical position, 'Emotivism' or 'Intuitionism', which holds that moral values are not rationally explicable but rather instinctive.

In many instances, perhaps the majority, people are applying the philosophical approach called 'Utilitarianism', which is almost universally at work in moral discussions today. This sees moral judgements as the product of an analysis of the foreseeable results of one's action. If an action is going to cause more pain and unhappiness than pleasure and happiness, then it is wrong. If it will, on the whole, produce happiness and pleasure then it is good. This too is an important aspect of what is involved. A person who made a decision without considering the pain that it would cause to others would be callous and irresponsible.

Still others are seeking to apply moral rules – the Ten Commandments or the rules they have been taught as part of their moral education. This reflects another aspect of the truth, namely, that morality means acting according to the mind of God.

The fact is that most people are operating a combination of approaches without any clear idea about how they differ, how they might be reconciled and to what extent these approaches are adequate. People will not have much difficulty in agreeing about slavery and torture and exploitation. But this may only disguise the fact that they are asking different questions – the first about his or her own feelings, the second about identifiable and, to some extent measurable, consequences, the third about what the Bible or some other guide lays down.

The limitations and temptations of each of these approaches are obvious enough. Any one of them taken on its own can lead to an impoverishment of our vision. Morality is not just about feeling at peace about one's actions; some moral decisions are difficult and disturbing to make. Morality is not just about the results our actions bring about, but also, for instance, about what they reveal about us and express about our attitude to others. There is more to acting morally, that is in accordance with the mind of God, than simply applying rules. As the *Catechism of the Catholic Church* puts it: 'The commandments properly so-called come in the second place: they express the implications of belonging to God through the establishment of the covenant. Moral existence is a response to the Lord's loving initiative'.[5]

In order to understand them properly and to develop a fuller understanding of the moral call, we need to place each of these approaches in the context of a wider vision.

The ARCIC Statement, *Life in Christ*, expressed that vision in this way:

> The true goal of the moral life is the flourishing and fulfilment of that humanity for which all men and women have been created. The fundamental moral question, therefore, is not, 'What ought we to do?', but 'What kind of persons are we called to become?' For children of God, moral obedience is nourished by the hope of becoming like God (cf I Jn 3: 1-3).[6]

The same point is made in the Pope John Paul's encyclical, *Veritatis splendor*, when he speaks of the rich young man who asked Jesus, 'What must I do to possess eternal life?' In the rich young man, he says, we recognise every person who, consciously or not, approaches Christ the Redeemer and asks about morality:

> For the young man, the question is not so much about rules to be followed, but *about the full meaning of life*. This is in fact the aspiration at the heart of every human decision and action, the quiet searching and interior prompting which sets freedom in motion. This question is ultimately an appeal to the absolute Good which attracts us and beckons us; it is the echo of a call from God who is the origin and the goal of human life.[7]

The danger is that we can begin to take the amazing core of our faith, and the promise it offers about the full meaning of life, for granted. At the Synod of Bishops for Europe, which I attended this autumn, I was very struck by a story told by an Indian bishop. He told of an old Hindu man who was very impressed by all the great work that Christian missionaries were doing in the field of education and health care and community development. He decided that he would like to know more about Christianity. So he asked the local priest, who gave him a copy of the Gospels. The man read with great interest for several days, coming back to comment on and discuss the teaching and the miracles of Jesus. Then one day he came, hardly able to contain his excitement. 'But it says here,' he said, 'that Jesus rose from the dead! This is the most amazing, marvellous news. This changes everything. Why did you not tell us?'

Maybe that is precisely what the world needs to hear – a moral vision that sees life as the pilgrim way, by which we follow Jesus Christ, through the power of the Holy Spirit, into the glory which he had with his Father before the world was made.

That is the context in which all our moral activity takes place:

> Created in the image of God, (human beings) are shaped by nature and culture, and participate in both the glory and the shame of the human story. Their responsibility to God issues in a responsibility for God's world, and their transformation into the likeness of God embraces their relationships both to the natural world and to one another. Hence no arbitrary boundaries may be set between the good of the individual, the common good of humanity, and the good of the whole created order. The context of the truly human life is the universal and all-embracing rule of God.[8]

That is a vision which sees our actions not just as producing this or that result in the short term, not just as obeying or violating a rule, not just as producing a sense of guilt or a sense of peace. It sees our actions as patterned by the power of the kingdom:

> The new humanity, which the Gospel makes possible, is present in the community of those who, already belonging to the new world inaugurated by the resurrection, live according to the law of the Spirit written in their hearts (cf. Jer 31:33). However, the Church has always to become more fully what its title-deeds proclaim it to be.[9]

In that perspective, the good action does indeed lead to happiness and fulfilment; it does indeed bring peace of mind; it does indeed accord with the will of God. That is the fundamental Christian perspective on morality, which we share. I am suggesting that we need to reflect seriously together, starting from that shared perspective, so that we can understand, if not always share, the conclusions that each of us draws from that common vision.

What *Life in Christ* calls 'our common vision of humanity in Christ' gives us the responsibility of deepening our common discernment to overcome the misunderstandings and differences which darken the moral wisdom we seek to share with the world.[10] The ARCIC document looks at a number of issues which divide the Catholic and Anglican Communions – in relation to divorce and contraception, homosexuality and abortion. While it does not go far towards resolving the differences, it shows how great is the underlying agreement even in these controversial issues:

> Anglicans and Roman Catholics do not talk to each other as moral strangers. They both appeal to a

shared tradition, and they recognise the same Scriptures as normative of that tradition. They both respect the role of reason in moral discernment. The both give due place to the classic virtue of prudence. We are convinced, therefore, that further exchange between our two traditions on moral questions will serve both the cause of Christian unity and the good of that larger society of which we are all part."

The lesson is wider than the two Communions who prepared the document: it is true also in the wider ecumenical context.

We are perhaps, as I suggested earlier, inhibited by the awareness that when we speak of the Scriptures and the Christian tradition, when we speak of our understanding of how humanity is saved in Christ, we are speaking as strangers to many people in that larger society.

I wish, therefore, to reflect a little on how we should see our moral reflection in the kind of society where the foundations of our common Christian vision are no longer the common currency of public discourse. A cartoon in the *London Times* on New Year's Day showed a speaker at the opening of the Millennium Dome being interrupted before he could say what event of 2000 years ago was being commemorated, because it is important not to 'upset the *religiously challenged*'!

A pluralism that would regard the mere expression of religious convictions as insulting to non-believers or to those of different beliefs would be a very odd expression of respect for plurality. Pluralism cannot mean that there is no objective truth, nor that we should pretend that the truth is unimportant. That would actually be destructive of real pluralism. The document *Freedom, Justice and Responsibility in Ireland*, prepared for the Irish Inter Church Meeting in 1997, says,

The pluralism which denies any absolute standard is mistaken not because it is too respectful of the opinions of every person but because it is not respectful enough. A person's honest convictions are worthy of the greatest respect, not because the outcome of the search for the truth is unimportant but because it is of the utmost importance. The human quest for understanding what is true and good and beautiful is, in its deepest significance, the search for the Creator of all. An approach which would say, in effect, 'Believe what you like, it is no concern of mine', is not compatible with a firm belief in the truth of the Gospel and a deep respect for the individual's search for meaning which culminates in the God who comes out to meet us.[12]

Chief Rabbi Jonathan Sacks[13] suggests that what we need to live in a multi-religious society is to be bilingual. We need to develop a common language of citizenship in which we try to express the shared values that make us a society and by which we try to build a more human society.

But we also need our native languages – the language of values and belief which we acquire in our families and churches and groups. It is this native language that gives the conviction and the vitality to the other and we neglect it at our peril. In isolation, the language of citizenship would be only a kind of Esperanto, with no real history or culture, and only the most tenuous roots in lived human experience.

There is much to be said in favour of liberal democracy, but it is not itself the source of the values on which it is built. A society where people's moral ideals looked no higher than to be good citizens of the State would live a rather impoverished community life.

We must not, of course, seek legal sanctions to endorse Christian moral values simply because they are Christian.

Neither should we too readily assume that the fact that something is regarded as important by some or all Christian denominations rules it out of consideration. Christian values in social matters are rarely exclusively confined to Christians. In any case, the issue for decision by law makers or social policy makers is not who holds a particular position but what is the likely impact of particular proposals on the common good of society.

On many public issues, there is no such thing as neutrality. It is not the case that remaining silent about our convictions is the best contribution we can make to society.

> The failure publicly to endorse these goals [e.g. life long marriage, the value of voluntary associations] is tantamount to asserting their unimportance.[14]

The truth of the matter is that we have a moral vision that is more true, more fully human, more liberating, more merciful, more full of promise, more noble, more saving, than any other. The most important contribution we can make to the good of our society is to strengthen and deepen that vision and communicate it more effectively. That is a major ecumenical challenge for the twenty-first century to grow in our understanding of that vision and in our ability to communicate it. Serious dialogue with one another is a vital element in that growth in understanding.

Notes

1. John Declaration on Justification, 31 October 1999, 42.
2. Cassidy, E., *Osservatore Romano*, Eng. ed., 24 November 1999.
3. John Paul II, *Redemptor hominis*, 10.
4. John Paul II, *Reconciliatio et paenitentia*, 18.
5. *Catechism of the Catholic Church*, 2062.
6. ARCIC, *Life in Christ*, Church House Publishing/CTS, London, 1994, n. 6.

7. John Paul II, *Veritatis splendor*, 7.
8. ARCIC, *Life in Christ*, 93.
9. *Life in Christ*, 20.
10. *Life in Christ*, 3.
11. *Life in Christ*, 102.
12. Department of Theological Questions, IICM, *Freedom, Justice and Responsibility in Ireland Today*, Veritas 1997, p. 43.
13. J. Sacks, *The Persistence of Faith*, Weidenfeld and Nicolson, 1991.
14. D. Walsh, *After Ideology*, Harper, 1990, p. 275.

Youth Ministry – Vision and Practice: A Church Response[*]

Communicating
The Second Vatican Council speaks about how God's self-revelation to the human race is passed on from generation to generation:

> What was handed on by the apostles comprises everything that serves to make the people of God live their lives in holiness and increase their faith. In this way the Church, in its doctrine, life and worship, perpetuates and transmits to every generation all that it itself is, all that it believes.[1]

In its full and proper meaning, therefore, youth ministry is not a particular specialised activity carried on by some members of the Church. It is the life of the Church, transmitting all that it is and believes to every generation. It

---

[*] An address delivered at All Hallows College, 21 February 2002.

is the organic growth of the Body of Christ renewing itself so that its life continues.

The passage goes on to point out another important factor in understanding this process. The message of the Incarnate Word has to take flesh in each generation. Transmission is not the whole story, as if a package were being passed on unopened:

> There is growth in insight into the realities and words that are being passed on. This comes about through the contemplation and study of believers who ponder these things in their hearts (cf. Lk 2:19, 51). And it comes from the intimate sense of spiritual realities which they experience. And it comes from the preaching of those who, on succeeding to the office of bishop, have received the sure charism of truth.[2]

All of these factors, including the role of the preacher, especially the bishop, are presented as being concerned not just with the preservation of the message but also with 'growth in insight into the realities and words that are being passed on'.

All that the Church is and believes has been received from the apostles and is passed on and received into a changing culture. The message will always acquire and retain something from the cultures into which it has been lived – the Biblical culture and all the cultures in which it has been expressed down the centuries.[3] By receiving and living the Gospel, each culture and each individual expresses it in some new way. It is not received passively, but is integrated by the receiver into his or her understanding of life and way of life. That integration is never complete. The Gospel is received into the lives of individuals and societies that remain in many ways alien to it. Part of the wonder and challenge of Christian faith is to recognise the Word incarnate in the limitations and the particularity of human flesh. The Gospel can only be heard in the limitations of human lives and human words. It can never be isolated from the culture in which it is spoken nor from the culture in which it is received. It is communicated in a kind of dialogue 'which inevitably becomes part of a certain dialogue of cultures'.[4]

The reception of what the Church is and what it believes cannot be merely passive because it concerns how we understand ourselves and how we understand the meaning of our lives. In revealing the Father and his love, the Second Vatican Council said, Christ also reveals the human being to him or herself.[5] In a passage in his first encyclical, Pope John Paul speaks of that process. To understand oneself fully, one has, he says, to 'draw near to Christ' with one's unrest, uncertainty, weakness and sinfulness. One must enter into Christ with one's whole self and 'assimilate the whole of the reality of the Incarnation and Redemption' in order to find oneself. This process bears fruit 'not only of adoration of God but of deep wonder at oneself'.[6]

Learning how greatly God loves us is the fundamental truth into which we are always only growing. That Good News is not something one merely receives like a piece of information. It is gradually learned when believers contemplate and study and ponder it in their hearts. It grows through the attempt to live its implications in relation to God, to one's fellow human beings and to all creation.

These thoughts are prompted by the sub-title that has been given to my lecture, 'A Church Response'. In one sense it could be seriously misleading. The Church cannot respond to youth ministry as if it were being done by someone else. One can go further and say that, far from being something to which the Church responds, youth ministry is the life of the Church perpetuating and transmitting what it is and what it believes.

So, if one is to use the phrase 'Church Response' at all, I would like to think of it not in the first place as the response of a bishop or of anyone else to the vision and practice of individuals who have a commitment to working with youth. Something much broader is involved. Youth ministry is not something to which the Church responds. Youth ministry is the response of the whole Church to the challenge of perpetuating and transmitting all that it is and all that it believes to a new generation.

The phrase 'youth ministry' can be misleading if one fails to see that what is involved is not, in the first instance, a matter for a particular group of experts. It is not first of all a task for ordained ministers or professionals or specialists. It is the organic process in which Christ's body grows and the belief and life of the Church is shared across the generations. Youth ministry is an integral part of the whole Church's life and mission.

This is not in any sense to play down the vital role that is played by so many people in helping to share the vision with young people through various forms of working with young people. I know the value of the work of the Catholic Youth Council here in Dublin. Since going to Limerick, I have been enormously impressed by the vitality and creativity of Muintearas Íosa (The Household of Jesus) and by the way in which so many of those who have experience of Muintearas are, years later, active in their parishes, in the diocese and further afield. A good deal of what I am going to say draws its inspiration from Muintearas. I know that this creativity and energy is paralleled in many other instances throughout the country.

I stress the point for this reason. We are reflecting on the self-communication of a community. We need to begin by being aware that *the whole community communicates*. This happens whether people like it or not, whether they are aware of it or not. It happens whether people think of themselves as engaged in youth ministry or not. It happens even when nothing is further from people's minds than youth ministry.

The question arises both about society in general and about the Church community in particular, 'What are we communicating to young people?' When I celebrate the sacrament of Confirmation, I say to the twelve-year-olds something like this: 'You are part of this Church community. We need you. Your gifts are important to us. We wish to encourage you to enter freely and creatively with us into our common task of living and sharing the Gospel of Christ. It is not just a matter of you making a commitment today. This community is supposed to be making a commitment to you, to recognise you as sharers in its life and mission.'

But is it just words? Am I telling the truth? I am convinced that it is more than words, because the clergy and the concerned parishioners are very clearly aware of and desperately anxious to involve young people in the life of the parish. When people are asked about pastoral priorities, the involvement of young people in the life of the parish is almost invariably the first item on the list. Every priest knows the refrain, 'What about the youth, Father?' When the phrase was spoken in a homily during a recent gathering of Limerick priests, the rueful smiles of recognition were immediate. But when one asks what should be done in order to achieve that goal, silence tends to reign! The Word is incarnate in a community of people who are limited, who are searching, who are often very well aware of their inadequacies. Yet in this very inadequacy the Mystery is revealed as well as concealed. The solution is certainly not to chase the illusion that one could create a community free of inadequacy and failure.

Spoken or unspoken, 'What about the youth?' is a familiar question, but it is not the first question. The first question is 'What is the life of our community actually communicating to its members and especially its young members?' Even more fundamentally, we need to ask 'How aware is the community that it is communicating and do the members understand the importance of that communication?' If not, the Christian community must face the challenge of becoming more effective in sharing what the Church is and what it believes. It is a challenge for each member, but those who are conscientised about the importance of youth ministry perceive it with particular clarity.

That question seems to lead on directly to a familiar concern of those who work with young people, whether in schools or in youth programmes, namely that the good experience they can have of the Church in those settings can be very hard to find replicated in their parishes. 'When I leave the school or the youth weekend, where is this community I have been experiencing and hearing about?' It is a serious concern. Its implications have been powerfully formulated by Pope John Paul:

> Catechesis runs the risk of becoming barren if no community of faith and Christian life takes the catechumen in at a certain stage of ... catechesis. That is why the ecclesial community at all levels has a twofold responsibility with regard to catechesis: it has the responsibility of providing for the training of its members, but it also has the responsibility of welcoming them into an environment where they can live as fully as possible what they have learned.[7]

Everybody working with youth is acutely aware of that risk of barrenness. They may even fear that the richer the experience of faith, worship and community in school or at youth gatherings, the greater is likely to be the disillusionment with the Church as it is perceived in the parish.

Tensions

The danger is that a good experience in the context of youth ministry may lead to an unrealistic and impossible idea about what it might mean to belong to a parish – a much larger and diverse gathering, consisting of people whose degree of involvement may vary from wholehearted to virtually undetectable.

There are tensions and challenges in belonging to a parish and to the wider church which do not exist in the same way or on the same scale in a youth group. These tensions are not all bad – they are an unavoidable part of a Church that is made up of people of every temperament and outlook. The tensions call us to a creative balance which is lifegiving.

It would be too simplistic to say that the parish is not doing its job and all that is required is to bring about renewal in the life of parishes. The reality is more complicated. Perhaps the most obvious sign that the reality is not so simple is that this sort of question does not arise simply in relation to the parish. Very similar concerns are expressed about the lack of involvement of young people in political affairs and what seems to be a lack of participation in social structures. There is, it would seem, something about the way that modern society works that does not attract or encourage people, and especially young people, to take responsibility and ownership in any structured way.

One source of this alienation is that we are too ready to see both society and the Church in terms of structures. If you ask any believer, young or old, about their parish, they will be likely to reply in terms of the visible, institutional elements rather than in the light of how members of the community actually live their faith.

The truth is that if we look at the average parish, there is far more going on within it than might often appear to its younger members. Indeed, there is more going on in a parish than is visible to anybody. What appears to a casual observer are the structures, the arrangements for religious services, the parish activities, groups and committees, the Catholic organisations operating with varying degrees of vitality, and so on. There may well be nobody who has an overall picture of everything that is going on even under these obvious headings.

These are, however, only the surface of parish life. The casual glance will take little account of the struggles and setbacks, the courage and commitment, the hopes and the heartbreaks, the anxieties and achievements, through which individuals and families draw strength and inspiration from their faith in Christ, nor will it see very much of the quiet support people offer one another through prayer and friendship and example.

Before asking what the life of our community is communicating, we need to reflect a little on what we mean by the life of the community. Perhaps it is not communicating as well as we might hope because it is being looked at in too narrow a perspective. One is usually not very far into the discussion of these questions before someone utters the phrase, 'the institutional Church'. It is a phrase that, generally speaking, can be taken to refer to an entity with which the speaker does not identify. It implies an entity that is the responsibility of some 'them' – the Pope, bishops, clergy, religious, the adults; it is a way of saying 'don't blame "us"; it is not our doing!' 'Institutional Church' is, in other words, a phrase that is almost invariably spoken 'from outside'.

But the tension between tradition and creativity, structure and spirit, doctrine and the search for truth, cannot be so dismissed by simply coming down in favour of creativity, spirit and searching. If either side of the tension is neglected, the integrity of the truth is lost. There is no point in being creative in a way that detaches one from the tradition that carries the message; just as there would be little point in sticking to the words of the tradition, while remaining untouched by the vibrant life which they express. It would be foolish to claim that one is guided by the Spirit if, at the same time, one is moving away from the Body of Christ, animated by the Spirit. It would be both arrogant and fruitless to search for the truth without realising that the truth has been sought and received and formulated by the generations that preceded us and has been heard by them in the community of the Church.

One might argue that, in relation to politics and economics a similar divorce between structure and its deepest meaning has happened. When we look at society, we tend only to see the State, the structures. The political system is regarded as the responsibility of politicians. Multinationals and financial forces unintelligible to most of us control the economic system. The tendency is to see these as being run by a 'them', who are increasingly mistrusted and resented. We are tempted to look on the society in which we live in much the same way as we are tempted to look at the Church and the parish – as an institution which we view 'from outside' and for whose shortcomings 'they' are entirely to blame.

The danger of this approach for the future of democratic societies is obvious. Democracy without participation would be a contradiction. One cannot live with integrity in a democracy while regarding political life as something of no interest or concern. To try to do so means opting out of a responsibility that one has simply by being a citizen:

> As authority is chiefly concerned with moral force, it follows that civil authority must appeal primarily to the conscience of individual citizens, that is to each one's duty to collaborate readily for the common good of all.[8]

There is a gap, therefore, between the structures and the spirit. The spirit is increasingly privatised and the structures are increasingly seen as merely structures. It is a recipe for a profound alienation from the structures, whether of Church or State. If structures are not seen as being at the service of a common vision, there can be no sense of belonging or participation.

There are all sorts of reasons for the alienation from structures that is evident in modern life – and is evident particularly among young people. One important reason is that modern societies are uncomfortable with the expression of deep religious and moral convictions. These are seen as private matters and as likely to be divisive for society. Another way of saying that is that modern societies encourage people to live on the surface.

Let us take the moral sphere for instance. We operate for the most part without coming face to face with the fundamental issue of the inequalities of our society and of the world. We do not like to think about that gap because it makes us uneasy and because we do not know what to do about it.[9]

Faced with this moral unease, there is an uncomfortable feeling that something fundamental is missing in our approach to political and economic issues. We feel that there are unaddressed issues below the surface.

In relation to religious questions, we operate for the most part, at least in our social lives, without ever adverting or referring to the question of the ultimate destiny of human life. Is the universe full of meaning or is it absurd? What happens after death? Is there a God to whom we are answerable and from whom we hope for fulfilment? Is Jesus Christ the ultimate revelation of God, God-with-us? We tend to think of the response to these questions as purely private matters. But that leads to the strange inconsistency whereby modern societies set out to discuss human rights or to develop an education system or to provide the conditions that will enable human beings to flourish without thinking that a clear picture of what a human being is or of the purpose of human life is in any way relevant to the enterprise.

If we do not face these basic questions, then we inevitably reduce the Church to its external elements. If it is not seen in terms of the mysterious, invisible and transcendent God, if it is not the context for a never ending pilgrimage towards God, then what is left but structures? The visible reality of the Church makes no sense unless it is seen as gathering real people with their real concerns into a common worship of God and a common life in Christ: 'Although the Church possess a "hierarchical structure", nevertheless this structure is totally ordered to the holiness of Christ's members'.[10]

That structure is necessary. The religious impulse expresses itself in the underlying restlessness of the human heart. Society is right to recognise that this powerful impulse can become dangerous and divisive. The history of persecutions and religious wars of cults and superstitions down the centuries makes it all too clear that religion can be distorted into a very destructive force: 'Spiritual energy is the hottest fire of all, and people who too naïvely play with that fire get burned'.[11]

The self-revelation of God is given to a people. It forms a people. The life of that people, its worship, its structures, its teachings carry the truth of that revelation and protect it from the distortions that would turn it into something destructive. Sometimes in history, the Church was slow to identify and correct aberrations. There has been violence and intolerance in what was supposed to be the service of the truth; there has been failure to show the true face of God, acquiescence in evil and oppression.[12] At the same time one can recognise what Chesterton called the 'whirling adventure' of the Church's history in which he sees 'the wild truth reeling but erect'.[13] If the Gospel had been lived only by enthused individuals, there is no doubt that it would have fragmented into an infinite number of superstitions.

It seems to me, therefore, that it is not very helpful to analyse the challenge of youth ministry simply in terms of thinking that the life of parishes should reproduce the heady chaos of a youth weekend. But neither is it simply a matter of inviting young people to become involved in a community that would be unaffected by their participation.

Céim a dó [Stage two]

The challenge for youth ministry was well expressed in a study of Muintearas Íosa – 'to allow and encourage young people to take ownership of their Church – a Church that they have chosen, in freedom, to care for; a Church that empowers them to make the world they live in a better place; a Church that guides them into and through a relationship with the God of Jesus Christ, a God who is madly, utterly and profoundly in love with all creation'.[14]

Over a quarter of a century ago, after a visit to Taizé, Fr Micheál Liston decided that 'we must offer young people an experience of the Church as gathering, freedom of expression, prayer, celebration, searching, community'.[15] These elements have been refined into what Muintearas calls the 'three fires', *Fáilte* [Welcome], *Foghlaim* [Learning], and *Guí* [Prayer].

The first necessity is that the young person is made to feel welcome and to share that gift of welcome with the others. Acceptance, 'whoever you are and whatever your doubts and failings', is what many young people hunger for. It is the first step towards a sense of belonging. Such an expression of unconditional love produced an extraordinary reaction when Pope John Paul said in Galway, 'Young people of Ireland, I love you.'

The second element is *foghlaim*, that is reflection and learning. We all need to grow through sharing the wealth of knowledge that is present not only within the group but in the richness of the Christian tradition, the scriptures, the lives of saints, the example and wisdom of people we have known, Christian art, the insights of previous generations into the mystery of Christ, expressed in doctrine, and in people's lives. Adulthood means, among other things, becoming aware of the shoulders on which we stand. Cicero said that to remain ignorant of what happened before you were born is to remain always a child.

Finally, there is *guí* [prayer]. The world in which young people are growing up, and in which we all live, is marked by a certain deafness to the mystery of God. Therefore, sharing in prayer is more necessary than it was in the past:

> Prayer needs community if it is to be nourished by real life and if it is to change and remain relevant to a young person's development ... Groups and places of prayer fill the hunger for prayer and interiority among young people. This hunger is sometimes unnoticed, as the pace and bustle of today's life hides people's interior hungers and thirsts from them.[16]

It is important that this is seen as offering an experience of *the Church*, not merely of the group that is gathered. It is an experience that should give a sense that the Church is not a mere structure but that it is the Body of Christ. Youth ministry must in the last analysis *be* the life of the Church, or it is not true to itself. It does not end with the deepening of Christian faith in some young people. It is concerned with the Church renewing her life and existence from one generation to the next:

The renewal of the Church that is asked for by the needs of young people today involves the Christian community in a challenge to present herself to all as *'a place of welcome through exchange, dialogue and prayer'*.[17]

The challenge is not just to the adult Christian community but to the whole community:

In each area, in each parish, young people are called to play their part in this renewal and in this openness to each individual and his or her story.[18]

That is clearly too big an aim to be met by youth groups or youth weekends or youth retreats or religious education programmes alone. Many kinds of youth activity, by their nature, lose their attraction as one grows older – for one thing, they become too exhausting! Every activity and environment in which the faith is communicated specifically to young people raises the question 'What next?' The question is regularly addressed in Muintearas under the heading *Céim a Dó* [Stage Two].

This is the fundamental challenge of youth ministry. Although it may only become apparent when someone 'grows out of' specifically youth-centred activities, it is crucial all along. It is the challenge of seeing this ministry as an integral part of the life of the wider community. The central point I am trying to make might be put under two headings.

First of all for those engaged consciously and explicitly in youth ministry: *It is not possible effectively to engage in youth ministry on the basis that what the wider community communicates is somebody else's business – or somebody else's fault. It is not possible effectively to engage in youth ministry except by taking some responsibility for the welcome and learning and prayer that is the life of the wider community.*

Secondly for each member of the community: *If young people find* fáilte, foghlaim agus guí *only in youth groups and activities then the community – and each member of it – needs to ask itself what it is communicating. Failure to communicate is not the result of bad will, but of a combination of factors such as fear and inability to see what is required. In combating those factors, people who have experience of youth ministry in the narrower sense have a vital role in helping the whole Church to enrich that essential dimension of its life.* I believe that the time might be ripe now for progress in awakening that awareness. In all sorts of ways the nature and the urgency of the challenges we face are becoming clearer to an increasing number of people in our parishes.

During their years of involvement in Christian youth activities, it is important that young people should have been encouraged to play their part in the renewal of their parishes in various ways. Their participation in liturgy and prayer groups, the activities they have undertaken in the social field, are all contributions to the life of the parish. More fundamentally every enrichment of their own faith is, *in itself*, an enrichment of the community. We are not by any means starting from zero.

The challenge for youth groups and gatherings is to retain a consciousness that they are part of the larger life of the Church. The absence of openness and welcome and of opportunities for creative dialogue between the generations, which young people often complain of in the parish, can have its parallel in youth groups. To be true to itself every facet of the Church's life must be missionary – that is, it must be open to the rest of the Church and to the wider world.

When young people who have been deeply involved begin to move away from youth-centred activities, it is often because they are no longer young. Late night sing songs and sleeping bags and campfire meals begin to lose their appeal.

That means a change of perspective, which needs to be addressed. It is not correct for young adults – indeed it never was – to be seen as a group contributing to the parish from a distance, as if they were not an organic part of the parish already. When they were younger they might, however, reasonably have felt that it was not realistic to expect schoolchildren to remedy a lack of opportunities for *fáilte, foghlaim agus guí*, in the life of the parish.

Moving away from youth-centred activities thus produces two challenges. The first is to find some way of continuing to be welcoming, searching, prayerful people without the familiar supports. The second is the realisation that there is nowhere to point the finger for the shortcomings of the adult community. *Céim a dó*, that is some kind of continuing contact among those who have had a good experience of the Young Church, is important in order to try to strengthen and live the vision. It is also important in order to retain a sense of the kind of community they would have wished to see in their parishes when they were younger and to consider what they can do to build such a community now, so that their own children will feel welcomed and needed and supported.

That is the clear challenge for young people when 'we' discover that we have become part of 'them'. The process of becoming an adult in the Church as in any community is the gradual realisation that there is no 'them', only 'us'. That realisation will dawn most effectively in the context of an experience of a parish that has always seen its young members as part of the wider 'us', where the welcome and the challenge have always been there. This goes right down to the welcoming smile rather than the disapproving look for teenagers who come to church looking very much like teenagers. It expresses itself in a willingness to take seriously the views of young people. It is a challenge for each person in the parish.

Both youth leaders and young people need a sense of responsibility to the whole community and for the whole community. If it does not try to develop that sense of responsibility and belonging, youth ministry is not true to its essential nature.

There will always be complaints, often valid complaints, about structures. These might range from disagreements about the timetable for Masses or plans for church alterations, to the blocking of pastoral initiatives or a lack of encouragement for them. Structures can be frustrating, but without them there is no living, continuing community. *Céim a dó* needs to be able to rise above the never completely avoidable frustrations of living in a structured society with others. *Céim a dó* is a commitment to the Church as the Body of Christ, with all its imperfections. The other members of the parish are not handpicked to suit me:

> A parish-type family is a hand of cards that is randomly dealt to us, and, precisely to the extent that it is truly inclusive, will include persons of every temperament, ideology, virtue and fault ... Church involvement, when understood properly, does not leave us the option to walk away whenever something happens that we do not like. It is a covenant commitment, like a marriage, and binds us for better or worse.[19]

The tensions of living with others in an inclusive family, the tensions between structures and the spirit, tradition and creativity, doctrine and search, are expressions of the one life, without which them the life cannot transmit itself from generation to generation.

One rises above these tensions in two ways. First of all by a constructive willingness to work with and improve the organised, visible life of the community in its role of supporting the growth in sharing of Christ's life – which is its only ultimate purpose. Secondly, it is important not to attribute to these external things a significance and a role that they can never have. The inadequacy of institutions cannot defeat the growth of the kingdom and their improvement cannot ensure it. The future of God's kingdom does not depend on such issues being resolved as I would wish. Every community will have disagreements, and some will be heated. But the Church is about more fundamental realities beside which the composition of the Parish Council, or particular pastoral initiatives, important as they are, should be seen with a certain sense of perspective. The whole point of the parish, in its visible organisation and in its inner life, is to be filled with the spirit of Christ:

> As the chosen of God, then, the holy people whom he loves, you are to be clothed in heartfelt compassion, in generosity and humility, gentleness and patience. Bear with one another; forgive each other if one of you has a complaint against another. The Lord has forgiven you, now you must do the same. Over all these clothes, put on love, the perfect bond (Col 3:13,14).

That is the life that the Church lives from generation to generation. Because that is the heart of youth ministry, it follows, I believe, that youth ministry cannot be considered without *céim a dó*. *Stage Two* simply means finding ways to encourage everyone, and especially those members who have had a good experience of the youth-dimension of the community's life, to accept the responsibility of being *the community which communicates*.

This is not some kind of optional follow-on to youth ministry but an ongoing commitment to the 'dialogue of cultures' which is at its heart. It describes the common responsibility and commitment of all of us, young or old, to enabling our flawed and imperfect Christian communities to communicate the truth of Christ:

> It is therefore necessary that at each moment of [the Church's] history the rising generation should in some way fulfil the hope of the preceding generations, the very hope of the Church, which is to transmit without end the gift of God, the Truth and the Life. This is why in every generation young Christians must ratify with full consciousness and unconditionally, the covenant entered into by them in the Sacrament of Baptism and reinforced in the Sacrament of Confirmation... We think that we have every reason to have confidence in Christian youth: youth will not fail the Church if within the Church there are enough older people able to understand them, to love them, to guide them and to open up to them a future by passing on to them with complete fidelity the Truth which endures. Then new workers, resolute and fervent will, in their turn enter upon spiritual and apostolic work in the fields which are white and ready for the harvest.[20]

Notes

1. Vatican II, *Dei verbum*, 8.
2. *Dei verbum*, 8.
3. cf. John Paul II, *Catechesi tradendae*, 53.
4. *Catechesi tradendae*, 53.
5. Vatican II, *Gaudium et spes*, 22.
6. John Paul II, *Redemptor hominis*, 10.
7. *Catechesi tradendae*, 24.
8. John XXIII, *Pacem in terris*, 48.
9. John Paul II, *Dives in misericordia*, 11.
10. John Paul II, *Mulieris dignitatem*, 27.
11. R. Rolheiser, *Seeking Spirituality*, London 1998, p. 29.
12. cf. John Paul II, *Tertio millennio adveniente*, 35, 36.
13. G. K. Chesterton, *Orthodoxy*, ch. VI.

14. N. Lynch, *Muintearas Íosa, Eaglais Óg nó Eaglais Eile,* (unpublihed) 1995.
15. M. Liston, 'The Emerging Church (1)', in *Resource,* Spring 1983, p. 19.
16. D. Neary, 'Young People and Prayer', *Mustard Seeds,* Veritas 1985, 71.
17. John Paul II, Opening of International Youth Centre, Rome 1983.
18. M. Liston, 'The Emerging Church (4)', *Resource,* Winter 1983, pp. 14, 15.
19. R. Rolheiser, *Seeking Spirituality,* p. 58.
20. Paul VI, *On Christian Joy* (1975), VI.

Signs of Discord, Seeds of Hope

The title given to this reflection, like many good titles, could mean a number of different things. It might be taken to imply that we should regard signs of discord as being necessarily in opposition to seeds of hope. I would prefer to take it as implying that signs of discord can themselves be seeds of hope. Alexander Pope wrote:

> All nature is but art unknown to thee;
> All chance, direction which thou canst not see;
> All discord, harmony not understood;
> All partial evil, universal good:
> And, spite of pride, in erring reason's spite,
> One truth is clear, whatever is, is right.[1]

It may be that signs of discord point towards new harmonies that we need to achieve in ourselves and in our society. They may spur us towards discovering and creating those new harmonies. It might be that tensions, frustrations and discords are what we need to urge us on to engage in the quest for harmony.

William James, physiologist, psychologist and philosopher (1842-1910), suggested as much in speaking about scientific advances:

> Without an imperious inner demand on our part for ideal logical and mathematical harmonies, we should never have attained to proving that such harmonies lie hidden between all the chinks and interstices of the crude natural world. Hardly a law has been established in science, hardly a fact ascertained, which was not first sought after, often with sweat and blood, to gratify an inner need.[2]

I want to suggest that this imperious inner demand operates in a wide range of areas.

Take, for instance, the challenge of prosperity and alienation. We face the challenge of living in the new and largely unanticipated environment which developed in Ireland during the final decades of the twentieth century. In the kind of economic, social and cultural transformation through which we are living, what may have been, or may have seemed to be, a harmonious balance has begun to break up. Our perspectives have been disrupted. The picture that we had of our world, of its direction and meaning, and of our place in it, needs to be adapted to the new situation. Things have changed, changed utterly, but the terrible beauty is still waiting to be born!

Another way of saying that is that we are in danger of losing our bearings in the unfamiliar terrain. In perhaps the most telling image of his Irish visit, and one which has become increasingly apt in the intervening years, Pope John Paul compared our situation to living in a new continent:

> The task of renewal in Christ is never finished. Every generation, with its own mentality and characteristics

is like a new continent to be won for Christ. The Church must constantly look for new ways that will enable her to understand more profoundly and to carry out with renewed vigour the mission received from her Founder.[3]

No generation can rest satisfied with the synthesis developed by its parents and grandparents because each new generation has to live in a different world. As a new century begins, we are experiencing the dramatic nature of the new continent more inescapably than many other generations have done. One of the most important seeds of hope is that we are a generation that can hardly fail to see that the challenge of making the Gospel take flesh has to involve looking for new ways, more profound understanding, renewed vigour.

Our generation, like every other and more than most, has to carry the Gospel into unfamiliar territory, and express it in a new language. That is an uncomfortable challenge, but it is also the process by which we can rediscover the freshness and the wonder of the truth.

No other generation has experienced the world that is opening up before us – a world of unimaginably complex and accessible communications, a world of huge scientific and technological advances, many of them raising major ethical questions, a world whose climate and natural resources are vulnerable in ways that no one previously imagined.

The question for us is this: Is it possible to have an overarching vision of meaning within which to make sense of this extraordinary present and the unknowable future? In particular can Christian faith provide that vision for our generation as it has for the generations that went before us?

We are in danger of 'information overload', indeed of a general 'stimulus overload', in a way that was never before the case. The issues that press in on us may often lack the intensity of the constant struggle for survival that was the lot of many of our ancestors; but we are bombarded by an extraordinary range of concerns that seem unconnected and infinitely varied.

Many people would admit to feeling swamped by demands and stresses, by a deluge of information, by moral uneasiness about injustice in the world, by pressures to conform to other people's expectations while longing to be one's own person, by feelings of powerlessness in the face of vast problems and by a fear that one does not really count in the great scheme of things – if there is a great scheme of things. We feel a great need to 'prioritise' and to 'focus', because life seems so unmanageable. Many of us find that our experience at least occasionally resonates with Yeats's line: 'Things fall apart; the centre cannot hold'.[4]

In its own way, this sense that life is becoming unmanageable is an expression of a need to rebuild the centre which will hold things together. Pope John Paul says that alienation involves 'a reversal of means and ends'.[5] In other words, secondary things come to be seen as primary; partial truths begin to be taken for the whole; we lose sight of the big picture; we do not know who we are or where we are going:

> It has happened therefore that reason, rather than voicing the human orientation towards truth, has wilted under the weight of so much knowledge and little by little has lost the capacity to lift its gaze to the heights, not daring to rise to the truth of being ...

....

Perspectives on life and the world, often of a scientific temper, have so proliferated that we face an increasing fragmentation of knowledge. This makes the search for meaning more difficult and often fruitless. Indeed, still more dramatically, in this maelstrom of data and facts in which we live and which seem to comprise the very fabric of life, many people wonder whether it still makes sense to ask about meaning.[6]

The question of meaning arises first of all about our own lives. 'Who am I? Who are we? Where does our life lead?' A person is alienated to the extent that his or her life is not perceived as bearing any relationship to these fundamental questions. Karl Marx described work as alienating because, while at work, the worker felt 'outside himself', 'not at home'. The most basic alienation is not being in touch with one's own deepest self.

In our kind of societies that kind of alienation seems inevitable. For a great part of our lives we are in contexts where the deeper aspects of ourselves seem irrelevant. Our family relationships, our religious convictions, our cultural interests are all part of our 'private lives' and of little or no concern to the people with whom we spend a great deal of our time. We pass most of our day with people who are in some sense strangers. We are not deeply involved with them. We are not fully present to the other person, and we are, therefore, not fully present to ourselves.[7]

That is the root of what Henri Nouwen calls the great paradox of our time – namely, that many of us are busy and bored at the same time:

> While we can hardly keep up with our many tasks and obligations, we are not so sure that it would make any difference if we did nothing at all. While people keep pushing us in all directions, we doubt if anyone really cares. In short, while our lives are full, we are unfulfilled.[8]

The busyness of our world is clear, not only in the pressures of work but also in the unending stream of noise and images and data, the constant transitions between unrelated areas of concern, the speed of communications, the huge concentrations of population and traffic in a modern city.

The fundamental question is not so much the amount and variety of activity – though that is clearly a problem – but the integration of it all into some intelligible pattern. As Ronald Rolheiser expressed it, 'Being filled, yet unfulfilled, comes from being without deep interiority'.[9]

But perhaps that discord is what can drive us towards a harmony that we have not yet understood. Teilhard de Chardin suggests, in fact, that it is necessary to feel the discord in order to know the harmony:

> One must have felt deeply the pain of being plunged into that multiplicity which swirls about one and slips through one's fingers if one is to be worthy of experiencing the rapture that transports the soul when, through the influence of the universal Presence, it perceives that reality has become not merely transparent but solidly *enduring*. For this means that the incorruptible principle of the universe is now and forever found, and that it extends everywhere: *the world is filled*, and filled with the Absolute. To see this is to be made free.[10]

Joy, says Teilhard, is the fruit of coming face to face with a universal enduring reality to which one can 'as it were attach' those fragmentary moments of happiness that, 'being successive and fugitive, excite the heart without satisfying it'.[11]

The discord between longing and fulfilment is the heart of the human condition. The human being is a restless quest. We long for what is infinite, eternal, perfect. But everything around us is limited, passing and flawed. Nothing we can possess, nothing we can experience, nothing we can achieve satisfies our longing.

Joy, and we might also say harmony, come through recognising the infinite in the finite, the universal in the particular, the eternal in the temporal, the spiritual in the material. That happens only when we recognise that we are ourselves a unity of finite and infinite, of unlimited longings and all too limited fulfilments. These are not two 'parts' of ourselves which we have somehow to 'stick together'. The human person is *one being* who is *both* everlasting *and* mortal, *both* limited *and* open to the transcendent. In separating these aspects, in failing to harmonise them, or in paying insufficient attention to one of them, we create discord within ourselves; we become alienated from ourselves.

We are not pure spirits imprisoned in alien matter. We are not two realities joined together, but one reality. We are embodied spirits. The human body is not just an instrument the person uses; it is the person existing and acting in the world. That is fundamental to the Christian understanding. If it were not the case, St John could not have made the extraordinary statement that the Word, who was God and by whom all things came to be, *was made flesh*.

That unity is the starting point but it is also the foundation of a permanently unfinished struggle to become more fully the unity which we already are. Kathleen Norris, in *The Cloister Walk*, quotes a monk who spoke of 'poetry's ability to draw together sacred and secular, back to the oneness of it all that we Westerners split ... Monks should not see divisions'.[12]

That search for wholeness takes many forms – art, religion, psychology, the quest for scientific truth, commitment to justice – all of these in their own ways seek to develop and give expression to a vision of reality and of the meaning of human life. The quest for wholeness in each of these spheres is also, at the same time, a quest for the wholeness and truth of our own being. Art, religion, psychology, science and so on, all involve addressing the question of who we are.

One of the most basic reflections of the tension between the material/spiritual, temporal/eternal nature of the human being is the tension between nature and freedom. I would like to reflect on the discord that we find in ourselves as individuals and in our culture in the area of freedom and morality.

The heart of the encyclical *Veritatis splendor* is the importance of recognising the human being as a unity. The Pope repeatedly points to the danger that we begin by setting nature and freedom in opposition to each other:

> The penchant for empirical observation, the procedures of scientific objectification, technological progress and certain forms of liberalism have led to these two terms being set in opposition, as if a dialectic, if not an absolute conflict, between freedom and nature were characteristic of the structure of human history.[13]

Even those who respect the dignity of freedom, 'frequently conceive of freedom as somehow in opposition to or conflict with material and biological nature over which it must progressively assert itself'.[14]

Human freedom is not the same as the creative freedom of God. We cannot create our own universe. Our freedom acts precisely by choosing among possibilities which it finds already existing; it uses abilities which we can certainly acquire and develop and perfect but only on the foundation of abilities that are innate; it acts for reasons that suggest themselves either from our own inner restlessness or from the world around us. None of these is created out of nothing.

A person who would seek to act as if he or she were not situated in a reality that has to be understood and dealt with, is not free but deluded. Our freedom has to start from where we are – not from where we would like to be or where we imagine we are. Once we regard the situation in which we find ourselves as external to our freedom, as mere material to be manipulated, as an obstacle to be overcome, we are left with a freedom that seeks to free itself from its own situation. But the paradox is that it is that very situation which provides the possibilities, the abilities and the motives that make human freedom possible in the first place.

There is, of course a sense in which the material world, including our own bodies, limits us. Much more fundamentally, however, they provide the field of possibility within which we can choose and act.

The model of freedom struggling to conquer its context has a certain truth. It is not the whole truth, nor even the most important truth. That is clear from the fact that the highest exercises of human freedom are often those that are the fruit of harmony rather than those that see freedom as a struggle between discordant realities. The great artistic creations, the highest achievements in sport or literature, are not marked by a struggle against hostile material. The greatest artists or athletes are those who display such harmony with their own body and with the material that they use as to make the achievement look easy.

In any case, without that 'situatedness' human freedom is broken off from its foundations.

> A freedom which claims to be absolute, ends up by treating the human body as a raw datum, devoid of

any meaning or moral values until freedom has shaped it in accordance with its design. Consequently, human nature and the body appear as *presuppositions or preambles*, materially *necessary* for freedom to make its choice, yet extrinsic to the person.[15]

That false idea of freedom involves a false idea of the human person. The real problem about regarding nature and freedom as being essentially in opposition is that it means regarding the human person as made up of two distinct parts in opposition to each other – a free soul and a body which it 'uses'. This contradicts the unity of the human person:

> The spiritual and immortal soul is the principle of unity of the human being, whereby it [the human being] exists as a whole – *corpore et anima unus* – as a person.[16]

We might illustrate it like this: if one attempts to understand the human person by means of a chemical analysis of the human body, there will come a point where an entirely new perspective is needed if one is to arrive at a picture that is recognisably human. There is no way of deducing from the consideration of large quantities of water and smaller quantities of carbon, phosphorus and so on the possibility that these might be capable of the greatest human cultural achievements, relationships of love and loyalty, scientific discoveries.

In the same way, if one begins by looking at human activity as the manipulation of a material body and the shaping of a recalcitrant material world by some kind of free spiritual centre, there is no way back into a unified understanding of human freedom because 'it is in the unity of body and soul that the person is the subject of his/her moral acts'.[17]

To begin with a purely physical description, 'a finger tenses around a trigger; a bullet is discharged: a bullet strikes someone's head; someone dies', is to miss the essential point as far as morality is concerned: How far and in what way is all of this the product of a free moral choice? The whole point about a morally significant act is that somebody chooses it. That choice is not injected into a pre-existing purely physical event, rather the choice expresses itself in the freely chosen action.

That may sound somewhat abstruse, but it has very practical implications. If one thinks of freedom as pushing around material things, including one's own body, then it becomes much easier to think that the whole significance of the free action lies in the results it brings about. Freedom becomes a mechanism for producing results. Moral judgement becomes a matter simply of weighing up those results.

The difficulties of trying to make moral decisions primarily on the basis of consequences are well known; I do not intend here to enter into a detailed discussion of Utilitarian or Consequentialist approaches to morality.[18] I would also want to recognise, as indeed the Pope does, that there have been legitimate, necessary and nuanced investigations by moral theologians in these areas.[19]

My concern is rather to suggest that moving towards a deeper understanding of these questions points us towards the underlying factor in the contemporary moral discord which Pope John Paul went so far as to describe as 'the overthrowing and downfall of moral values'.[20] The deepest signs of discord are actually the discordant ways in which we understand ourselves; the seeds of hope are the challenge to understand ourselves in a more rounded and complete way.

Almost fifty years ago Frank Sheed wrote of the variety of different ways in which we understand ourselves as human beings, as matter, as spirit, as a union of both – and all the possible subdivisions of those positions:

> The people who admit the soul differ whether their will is free or not, and whether the intellect has valid knowledge, and indeed whether the phrase valid knowledge has any meaning, and if so what. The people who deny or disparage the body differ as to the practical consequences of their view; some say that the body should be ignored in the hope that if you don't look at it it will go away, some that it should be maltreated by an extreme asceticism so that it will fall away, some that as the body does not matter it does not matter what we do with it so that they can plunge into any sort of bodily indulgence with no detriment to their purity'.[21]

He goes on to reflect that it is unrealistic to think that people thus divided as to what a human being is could be capable of agreeing about how a human being should be treated.

A rounded view of the human person leads to a rounded view of the significance of human actions. There is more to a free decision than the choice between possible lines of action and the possible consequences that flow from them.

The human body is not just an instrument for producing results, it is an expression of the person and it is the possibility for the person's relating to other people and to the world. We speak about 'body language', but, in a much more fundamental sense, the human body is the language in which we communicate.

In every exercise of freedom, many dimensions are at work. Every free choice, at least implicitly, recognises or refuses to recognise one's own dignity and the dignity of other human beings who are affected by it. Since we are talking about a language, the first question is not about the consequences of what we 'say' but about its truth. If what an action says is not a true expression of the dignity of the person acting or of the persons affected, then it is immoral. Of course, as with every untrue statement, it is necessary to ask whether it is a deliberate lie or an honest mistake.

If we understand the unity of the human person, it means that a person's actions are not just something out there. My free actions *are myself* choosing and acting:

> It has been rightly pointed out that freedom is not only the choice for one or another particular action; it is also, within that choice, a decision about oneself and a setting of one's own life for or against the Good, for or against the Truth, and ultimately for or against God... Human acts are good or evil because the express and determine the goodness or the evil of the individual who performs them.[22]

That is why a thoroughgoing utilitarianism, which would see consequences as the primary, and even the only, criterion of morality would be inadequate – not just as an account of morality but as an account of human choosing.

The only path towards a resolution of the discord that marks moral discussion is to rediscover the unity and dignity of the human person. As Frank Sheed suggested, only if we can agree on what a human being is can we hope to agree on how a human being should be treated and on how a human being should act. The need to find ways to speak to one another on these issues is increasingly urgent in Western society. That urgency is a seed of hope.

The human being is one. The drive towards human fulfilment is a single dynamism, not, as it might often seem, a whole cacophony of competing and unrelated calls. We are more aware than ever before of the complexity of human existence. We are aware of the factors, conscious and unconscious, social and genetic, that influence human behaviour. But we also know in our hearts that we are a single longing for happiness and fulfilment.

That unity is the starting point of *Veritatis splendor*. It begins with the question of the rich young man, 'What must I do to possess eternal life?'

> For the young man, the question is not so much about rules to be followed, but *about the full meaning of life*. This is in fact the aspiration at the heart of every human decision and action, the quiet searching and interior prompting which sets freedom in motion. This question is an appeal to the absolute Good which attracts us and beckons us; it is the echo of a call from God who is the origin and goal of human life.[23]

We are talking here about the final end, which according to Aquinas, moves every human longing.[24] We are also talking about the conscience where, according to Vatican II, in the deep recesses of our being, God who probes the heart awaits us and we decide our own destiny in the sight of God.[25] The heart is described by the Catechism of the Catholic Church in these words:

> The heart is the dwelling place where I am, where I life ... the heart is the place 'to which I withdraw'. The heart is our hidden centre, beyond the grasp of our reason and of other people; only the Spirit of God can fathom the human heart and know it fully. The heart is the place of decision, deeper than our psychic drives. It is the place of truth, where we choose life or death. It is the place of encounter, because as image of God we live in relation. It is the place of covenant.[26]

The seeds of hope, in the moral sphere, as indeed in other spheres, artistic and scientific and political and psychological, depend on touching the heart where we can begin to discover harmonies not understood.

Notes
1. Alexander Pope, *Essay on Man*.
2. W. James, *Essays on Faith and Morals*, Meridian, 1962, p. 24.
3. John Paul II, Homily in Knock, 30 September 1979.
4. W. B. Yeats, The Second Coming.
5. John Paul II, *Centesimus annus*, 41.
6. John Paul II, *Fides et ratio*, 5, 81.
7. cf. G. Marcel, *Essai de Philosophie Concrète*, Gallimard 1967, p. 55.
8. H. Nouwen, *Making All Things New*, Doubleday 1981, p. 24.
9. R. Rolheiser, *The Shattered Lantern*, Hodder & Stoughton 1994, p. 42.
10. P. Teilhard de Chardin, *Hymn of the Universe*, Fontana 1970, pp. 89, 90.
11. Teilhard de Chardin, *Hymn of the Universe*, p. 89.
12. K. Norris, *The Cloister Walk*, Riverside, New York, 1996, p. 157.
13. John Paul II, *Veritatis splendor*, 46
14. *Veritatis splendor*, 46.
15. *Veritatis splendor*, 48.
16. *Veritatis splendor*, 48.
17. *Veritatis splendor*, 48.
18. cf. *Veritatis splendor*, 77, J. Finnis, *Fundamentals of Ethics*, Clarendon Oxford, 1983.
19. cf. *Veritatis splendor*, 74.
20. John Paul II, *Reconciliatio et paenitentia* 18.
21. F. Sheed, *Society and Sanity*, Sheed and Ward, 1953, p. 20
22. *Veritatis splendor*, 65, 71.
23. *Veritatis splendor*, 7.
24. Aquinas, *Summa Theologiae* I-II q.1, a.6c
25. Vatican II, *Gaudium et spes* 14.
26. *Catechism of the Catholic Church*, 2563.

Health Care – Serving Human Life

Reflections on Evangelium Vitae[*]

Denial of solidarity – denial of life
In the early sections of the encyclical *Evangelium vitae*, Pope John Paul reflects on the story of Cain and Abel. Cain tries to evade God's challenge by saying, 'Am I my brother's keeper?' In doing so, he shows, as the Pope puts it, that he 'does not wish to think about his brother and refuses to accept the responsibility which every person has towards others'.[1]

This refusal of responsibility in the first book of the Bible is paralleled in the reality of the contemporary world:

> This reality is characterised by the emergence of a culture which denies solidarity and in many cases takes the form of a veritable 'culture of death'. This culture is actively fostered by powerful cultural, economic and political currents which encourage an idea of society excessively concerned with efficiency.[2]

---

[*] First published in the *Catholic Medical Quarterly*, Vol. LI, No. 2 (292), May 2001.

It is significant that the Pope links the culture of death with the denial of solidarity. We can all too easily see in the world around us instances of violence against life – genocide, euthanasia, abortion, torture, slavery and so on. These are fruits of the culture of death. But we need to recognise that the deeper roots of the culture of death lie in a failure to appreciate the meaning of human life and the consequent failure to understand and live the solidarity which that meaning demands.

Often, I suspect, people's sense of the meaning of life is formulated on the basis of unexamined assumptions. It is easy, for example, to assume that our own cultural perspective is the only possible one and that it is an entirely objective standpoint.

Nowadays there is a widespread unexamined assumption that only science is capable of giving us the real, objective truth. It is also assumed that science demonstrates that a complete explanation of the origin of human life is to be found in the evolutionary process of the survival of the fittest.

This would mean that, however implicitly, one would see life simply as the fruit of a bitter, pitiless struggle. The life which survives is the one which has most efficiently conquered its environment and subdued its rivals. The development of life is the victory of the strong at the expense of the weak. Successful living in that perspective would mean the acquisition of power, status and resources. These, incidentally, are the very temptations that Jesus rejected in the desert!

That is not to say that scientific truth can be disregarded. But, in seeking to understand reality, what can be scientifically proved and measured is not necessarily the most significant truth. When a scientist tells us that a human being is made up for the most part of water, with some carbon, calcium and other elements in lesser quantities, we can acknowledge that this is a true answer to the question, 'What constitutes a human being?' But it is an answer from a very limited perspective. A deep understanding of the mystery of the human person will not be arrived at through an ever more sophisticated chemical analysis.

But as scientific information becomes more complex and impressive – for instance in the context of the human genome project – it is more tempting for people to believe that 'the fault, dear Brutus, lies not in our stars but in our genes'.

The gift of God and the call to communion
God is the source of all life. We may well recognise an evolutionary principle or drive set into creation by the Creator, which has led to the emergence of life in microbes and plants and animals. Human beings may be seen as part of that process, but that is not the whole truth, nor the most important truth, about human life.

Whatever light the theory of evolution, or indeed the study of the genome, may shed on human existence, an adequate understanding of the origin and meaning of human life needs to see it above all as a personal gift of God

The Catholic tradition teaches that each human being is brought into existence by a particular creative act of God: 'Every spiritual soul is created immediately by God'.[3] In that act, God makes the human person in his own image and likeness; God, who wishes all to be saved and come to a knowledge of the truth (I Tim 2:4), invites the human person to share in the divine life; God addresses the human person as a being created for his or her own sake.[4]

None of these statements refers exclusively, or even primarily, to the Christian, who shares in the divine life through Baptism. They are true of human beings simply as human. Every human being is immediately created by God, made in the image of God and called to salvation and to the knowledge of God's truth. To be human is to be individually addressed by that word of God.

The full significance of God's personal creation and call is revealed in Christ, not as something alien and foreign to the longings of the human heart, but as their fulfilment, a fulfilment entirely beyond any human capacity to achieve:

> The Church knows that this Gospel of Life, which she has received from her Lord, has a profound and persuasive echo in the heart of every person – believer and non-believer alike – because it marvellously fulfils all the heart's expectations while infinitely surpassing them.[5]

Human life, therefore, does not find its ultimate origin or meaning in struggle and competition. It is not to be claimed as a right that has been earned, or taken as a prize that has been won by conquest. It is to be received as a gift freely given. The goal of life is not a commodity in short supply; it is a share in the unlimited life of God. Thus, 'revelation teaches us that life in its origins is not the self-assertion of the fittest, but love; and that human beings are the image of this original life'.[6] The meaning of human life is found in love. It is only in self-giving that human beings can fully discover their true selves.[7] Successful living consists not in the acquisition of power, status and resources but in giving oneself.

That is why 'the emergence of a culture which denies solidarity' is so closely linked to the growth of a culture of death. To know that the meaning of human life is found in love is to know that solidarity is an essential element in human flourishing and that a refusal of solidarity is a refusal of life.

Without the solidarity of the human community, a person would not learn to speak, to be moral, or to love.

There could be no language if there were no one to speak to. There could be no morality as we know it if there were no interaction with other people. There could be no love if there were no one to love us and to be loved. Without the solidarity of the human community, there would be no fullness of human life.

The Golden Rule, which is found in many religions and cultures, demands that we see every human being as a person whom we should treat as we would wish to be treated ourselves. Christian revelation goes further:

> One's neighbour is then not only a human being with his or her own rights and a fundamental equality with everyone else, but becomes the *living image* of God the Father, redeemed by the blood of Jesus Christ and placed under the permanent action of the Holy Spirit... Beyond human and natural bonds, already so close and strong, there is discerned in the light of faith a new *model* of the *unity* of the human race, which must ultimately inspire our *solidarity*. This supreme *model of unity*, which is a reflection of the intimate life of God, one God in three Persons, is what we Christians mean by the word *'communion'*.[8]

Without the solidarity of the Christian community, a human being could not come to believe in the message of Christ. It is only through the scriptures and the living faith of the community that the Gospel is spoken in the world. 'How will they hear of him unless there is a preacher for them? And how will there be preachers if they are not sent?' (Rom 10:14,15) It is through the community of the Church, Christ's body, that we learn 'to see in every human face the face of Christ'.[9]

We are dependent on one another because every human being is vulnerable, fallible, mortal and ignorant of many things that he or she needs to know. It is not possible genuinely to respect the life of a human being, fallible and mortal like oneself, unless one is willing 'to accept the responsibility which every person has towards others'.

The commandment 'Thou shalt not kill' is not observed simply by refraining from murder. It indicates a minimum below which a free individual should never under any circumstances descend. But, from that minimum, people, 'must start out in order to say "yes" over and over again, a "yes" which will gradually embrace the *entire horizon of the good'* (cf. Mt 5:48)[10]:

> The commandment 'You shall not kill' thus establishes the point of departure for the start of true freedom. It leads us to promote life actively, and to develop particular ways of thinking and acting which serve life. In this way we exercise our responsibility towards the persons entrusted to us and we show, in deeds and in truth, our gratitude to God for the great gift of life (cf. Ps 139:13,14). The God of the Covenant has entrusted the life of every individual to his or her fellow human beings...[11]

The answer to Cain's question is that we are indeed responsible for one another.

A special relationship

The health care vocation has an honoured place in Christian tradition. But it should not be seen in isolation from the life of the whole Christian community. It is a particular response to the universal call to recognise that the God of the Covenant entrusts the life of each individual to all of us.

I want to reflect on *medicine, morals and the third millennium* in this wider context, which is the foundation for a Christian vision of health care. Health care is a particularly intense expression of the responsibility we have for one another. The patient entrusts his or her life to the doctor or the health care team in a way that makes that responsibility very explicit and immediate.

From the point of view of the patient this entrustment is often total. A sick person may feel utterly frightened and helpless and be suffering acutely, physically and mentally. Perhaps for the first time, the patient's life and future seem to have slipped out of his or her control. The patient is dependent and has to trust in others to a degree that, perhaps, they have not known since infancy. I believe it is vital, in all the discussions about the complicated issues that arise in bio-ethics today, that we do not lose sight of the underlying relationship of trust between patient and carer which is the foundation of all that is done in the name of medicine.

The new century will almost certainly bring utterly unanticipated changes both for good and for ill to the world of health care. Already, we may sometimes wonder whether our moral reflections may be missing the point because we are unaware of some new developments, already well advanced, that will pose far more significant ethical questions than the issues that currently occupy our attention.

The human genome project, for instance, will raise great moral challenges, but many of them are not yet discernible. Before the century is out, there may well be even more dramatic challenges arising from as yet unimagined breakthroughs. It is important, therefore, even as we look at the particular ethical issues of our own day, that we should also remain focussed on the underlying question of the meaning of health care. This in turn rests on an understanding of the meaning of human life and of human solidarity. These will remain the foundations on which our response to whatever the future brings should be based.

The unity of the person

The mention of the human genome project suggests that we look a little deeper. Even if it does not necessarily lead to the conclusion that everything in human consciousness and behaviour can be explained in terms of genes, it may subtly strengthen the idea that the human being is no more than a highly sophisticated machine. People may or may not suppose that this machine is driven by some kind of spiritual core. They may also have an idea that that, if that core does exist, it may be much less in control than it imagines.

The advances in computers and the dream of creating artificial intelligence may lead many to suspect that even what we think of as our spiritual core is nothing more than an extraordinarily sophisticated machine. They may feel that what we call the human spirit is no more than the product of particularly complex interactions of material elements and impulses.

One may often find, therefore, in contemporary thinking an attitude that regards the soul or spirit either as identical with the body or as a being quite detached and separate from the body – a 'real me', struggling to control this recalcitrant physical envelope.

This is not the reality of our experience or of our existence. A human body is not just one among the objects in the physical world. In one sense, of course, it is an object, with size and weight and shape. More significantly, however, it is a subject. For some human person, this physical body is 'I'.

'I' am not a sort of spiritual puppet-master hidden away somewhere deep in my brain; *I am a living body*. Anything that is done to my body is done to me; anything that is done freely by my body is done by me.

Some of the actions performed by this body are not done freely; they are just events in the world that follow the scientific laws of physics or physiology – like falling down or snoring. Other actions, however, from the point of view of the person, are 'my actions', expressing 'my choices', 'my values' and 'my attitudes'. The various limbs and organs of the human body are not just objects of anatomical study or diagnosis. 'My arms' and 'my heart' are part of what I mean by 'me'.

It is fundamental both for medicine and for morals, and therefore for bioethics, to recognise the unity of the human person. Medicine deals not with a machine attached in some mysterious way to a conscious core, or a machine which through some particularly complex physical processes produces consciousness, but with a person who is an embodied spirit.

The poignancy of the situations that doctors often have to deal with and the respect that is due to the patient both come back to this. The doctor's relationship is not merely with a physical body but with a person.

It can be tempting sometimes to see the patient as confined and trapped in an ailing body. But that is not the whole reality. It is also true, for instance, that he or she cannot even express that frustration except through and in that weak or damaged body, which is not a mere thing, separate from the patient. To try to divide the person into a totally free and healthy centre and a sick and imprisoning body does not do justice to the reality of human experience. It is not just the body which is sick but the person.

The person who has unlimited aspirations lives within the limitations of time and space and ability and, perhaps, of failing health. And yet the physical universe and the physical body are not just limitations, they are the only medium through which the unlimited longings and hopes can be expressed and experienced. They are also, we believe, the setting of our journey towards the fulfilment of our unlimited hopes.

Communication and communion

Part of that separation of the person and the body arises from a misunderstanding of what it means to be a person. Pope John Paul refers to a mentality that 'recognises as a subject of human rights only the person who enjoys full or at least incipient autonomy'; he also refers to 'the mentality which tends to *equate personal dignity with the capacity for verbal and explicit*, or at least perceptible, *communication*'. He points out that, if one follows these lines,

> ... there is no place in the world for anyone who, like the unborn or the dying, is a weak element in the social structure, or for anyone who appears completely at the mercy of others and radically dependent on them, and can only communicate through the silent language of a profound sharing of affection.[12]

The reference to 'perceptible communication' is interesting. Communication and relationships are more than verbal communication. 'Communication is more than the expression of ideas and the indication of emotion. At its most profound level, it is the giving of self in love'.[13]

The discussions on the status of the embryo and when life begins focus our attention on the individual human being in the womb, or indeed in the test tube. We rightly point to the particular genetic make up of this unique individual.

But he or she is more than an individual. The tendency of our culture is to be very individualistic. Perhaps that can lead us to forget another essential aspect of the human person. To speak of a human being is to speak of already existing relationships. Every human being is a member of what we describe as 'the human family'. More concretely, one cannot be a human being without being a son or daughter, a grandson or granddaughter, and possibly also a niece or nephew, a brother or sister, or a cousin.

Long before we could speak or be conscious, we were caught up in relationships that were a part of our identity from the very beginning and that would remain part of our identity forever. The human response of love and recognition, communication in the narrow sense, does not simply begin when a baby speaks for the first time. That first verbal communication is a response to a relationship that began to exist as soon as this son or daughter was conceived.

The deep urge in many people to seek out their birth parents whom they never knew, testifies to this sense of a relationship that exists even if it was never consciously expressed.

Communication has its source and its goal in the unity of the human race with its Father and Creator. The word that God speaks to each new human being in the act of creation is already a word spoken to a being in community. The human being is an image of God not just because of his or her intellect and free will, but through the community of persons in which we were created from the beginning. 'So God created humankind in his image, in the image of God he created them; male and female he created them' (Gen 1: 27):

> He has willed to make women and men holy and to save them, not as individuals without any bond between them, but rather to make them into a people who might acknowledge him and serve him in holiness.[14]

On a wider scale, to speak of a human being is to speak of someone called to be part of the family of God, united in truth and love in a way that resembles the union existing among the divine persons[15]:

> In affirming that the spouses, as parents, cooperate with God the Creator in conceiving and giving birth to a new human being, we are not speaking merely with reference to the laws of biology. Instead, we wish to emphasise that *God himself is present in human fatherhood and motherhood* quite differently than he is present in all other instances of begetting 'on earth'. Indeed God alone is the source of that 'image and likeness' which is proper to the human being, as it was received at Creation. Begetting is the continuation of Creation.[16]

The fact that the development of an embryo may be still at a very early stage, the fact that a severe congenital condition may seriously restrict that development, the fact that a person may never again be capable of conscious interaction with others, does not negate that call of God, or that relationship to the human family. Every living human body is a person, a member of the human community and of the family of God.

The core and the consequences

When the Pope identifies the core of the Gospel of Life, he speaks, as we have been doing, of communion, bodiliness, relationship and the gift of self. The core of the Gospel of Life is:

> ... the proclamation of a living God who is close to us, who calls us to profound communion with himself and awakens in us the certain hope of eternal life. It is the affirmation of the inseparable connection between the person, his life and his bodiliness. It is the presentation of human life as a life of relationship, a gift of God, the fruit and sign of his love. It is the proclamation that Jesus has a unique relationship

with every person, which enables us to see in every human face the face of Christ. It is the call for a 'sincere gift of self' as the fullest way to realise our personal freedom.[17]

These are the concepts that guide us in looking at the consequences for health care of the basic questions that face us: How can we ensure that health care is in harmony with the culture of life? Can we be alert to the dangers that could draw it into the culture of death?

Not institutions but communities

We might approach those questions by looking at some of the consequences that the Pope himself draws from the Gospel of Life. One of these consequences is that respect for life requires that science and technology should always be at the service of the human person and of the person's integral development.[18] Health care at its most fundamental is a relationship between persons. One of the priorities in the new century will be to maintain that sense of personal service.

The challenge that faces us as research expands our knowledge and medical technology becomes ever more complex and specialised, is to try to ensure that the person of the patient does not get lost. We have all seen very capable and self-assured people becoming passive and helpless in the unfamiliar and frightening context of a hospital. Indeed the hospital can sometimes look to an incoming patient like an awesomely complicated institution that would run much more smoothly if it were not for all the sick people who get in the way!

We are all aware of the danger that the distress and uncertainty of an individual might be neglected while overworked health care personnel struggle to bring their particular professional expertise to bear on 'their' aspect of the patient's problem. We have all heard stories of the wise old GP who makes a correct diagnosis at first glance when batteries of tests have failed to do so because the tests were not looking for the right thing!

The drive for efficiency in the provision of health care is inevitable and right, given the vast amounts of public money that are spent. But I sometimes wonder whether the efficiencies are always calculated with a real understanding of the nature of health care.

Medical people complain that administrators do not understand the strictly medical issues. That may sometimes be true, but I have a broader concern. Even in terms of efficiency, the speed of recovery, reducing bed-nights and so on, what would be the effect of ensuring that each patient in a hospital could be sure that someone on the health care team really had the time to listen to his or her worries and to understand them? In the past, nurses seemed to have very much more freedom to sit and listen. To the extent that this has been eroded, I suspect that the system may have become less efficient, even in statistical terms.

Like other institutions in society – such as the churches, politics and education – medicine suffers from a generalised distrust and alienation. If this continues to grow the very cohesion of society will be at risk.

An underlying feeling of detachment can easily become hostility when people see real flaws and failures in the institution or in its 'professional' personnel – child abuse, organ retention, irregular political donations.

People may well approach health care with a sense of alienation. The hospital is seen as an institution doing things to and for the patient, but the patient does not expect to play any active or responsible part in the process. There may well be a feeling that his or her needs and anxieties do not count for much in the functioning of this huge structure. If that is the case, there is something fundamentally wrong.

The idea that the patient plays no part in the process of healing is quite false:

> The bodily, instinctual, psychological and spiritual ego of the patient is an active part of the reconstruction of the lost well-being.[19]

This, presumably, is what is at work in the placebo effect, when a patient's condition improves even though nothing has been done that would explain the improvement.

The hospital should rather be a community, in which the patient believes that his or her feelings and anxieties count. The sick person should be able to feel that he or she is seen as a person and not just as a case or a collection of symptoms. This involves, as the Pope put it, openness to the patient's interiority, world, psychology and culture. It 'involves a simultaneous giving and receiving, that is the creation of that communion which is total participation'.[20]

The challenge that this poses, as scientific and technological advance continues apace, is an uncomfortable one. I will put it very bluntly in the words of a man who has spent his life in health care, Pierluigi Marchesi, former Prior General of the St John of God Brothers:

> To humanise a hospital – or, rather, introduce into the hospital the dimension of humanity, understanding, respect, and response to the patient's needs and motivations – means that all health professionals must seek continual improvement – a kind of leap which few universities have proposed, beyond the arrogance of power and so-called scientific knowledge, to plunge into a process of identification with the suffering individual, a process which enables us to comprehend before acting and give rise to hope, trust, and a therapeutic partnership.[21]

The incomparable value of every human person[22]

Another consequence of the Gospel of life is that, 'Human life, as a gift of God, is sacred and inviolable'. 'Society as a whole must respect, defend and promote the dignity of every human person, at every moment and in every condition of that person's life'.[23] 'Human life is sacred because from its beginning it involves 'the creative action of God', and it remains forever in a special relationship with the Creator who is its sole end... no one can, in any circumstance, claim for himself the right to destroy directly an innocent human being'.[24]

Wherever one is faced with a living human being, one is faced with an inviolable life. Sometimes we may be tempted to use words which disguise this reality. At the end of life, while the patient is not yet dead, it is not right to say, 'he is only a vegetable; she is only a shell'. The human person is a living body. *If the body is living, the person is living.* The person is not some guiding force inside the body which might have slipped away, leaving the body like a driverless car with the engine ticking over. At the beginning of life it is not right to say, 'this is only a collection of cells; this is just the product of conception'. When a human life has begun, it is God's gift; he or she is a unique individual. This life is of more value than many sparrows (Mt 10: 31); it is more valuable than anything in the inanimate universe.

The encyclical specifically points to two major issues in defending the inviolability of human life in our world – abortion and euthanasia. The Holy Father condemns them in the most specific terms.[25] There is no need in this gathering to point to the enormous scale of the destruction of human life through abortion. There is every reason to fear that euthanasia will pose a steeply increasing challenge in the years ahead. Already, one country in the European Union has made it legal.

In both cases, abortion and euthanasia, we need to stress that there can be no such thing as degrees of belonging to the human family. Either a being is human or it is not. If a life which has the potential to blossom into consciousness and ultimately into eternal life has begun, then we must treat that living being as member of the human family. This remains true even if there are controversies and questions about the precise moment when the life of a person begins:

> Respect for human life is called for from the time that the process of generation begins. From the time that the ovum is fertilised, a life is begun which is neither that of the father nor of the mother; it is rather the life of a new human being with his or her own growth. It would never become human if it were not human already.[26]

It is particularly important that we do not fall into the trap of thinking that the respect due to a particular person's life can be measured in proportion to the 'quality' of that life. One often notes that the concept of 'quality of life' is being used as a means for valuing lives. It is one thing to judge that a particular form of treatment is not worthwhile because it will achieve little for the patient or is likely to be more harmful than beneficial. It is quite another to judge that a person's life is not worthwhile or not worth saving, because it is of such poor quality.

Obviously, in making the former decision, one of the considerations will be to ask what the treatment is likely to be achieved for the patient in terms, for instance, of conscious, pain-free, independent, active life. But that consideration is legitimate only in deciding whether the *treatment* will yield worthwhile benefits to the patient, not in deciding whether the patient's life is worthwhile. A human life is always worthwhile.

Begotten or made?
It is very likely that the new century will bring a whole range of new questions about the inviolability of life. We will be faced not just with issues about taking life but also with issues about changing life.

The hope of curing genetically inherited diseases like cystic fibrosis or haemophilia through gene therapy is obviously greatly to be welcomed. If that could be safely done through germ-line therapy, so that these diseases were never passed on in the first place, so much the better. But it may not be that simple. Germ-line therapy raises very particular problems.

It is likely, before the century is very old, that we will be faced with the possibility of genetic therapy which would not just seek to eliminate disease, but would aim at 'perfecting' an individual in the area of intellect or memory, in the area of emotion or personality, or merely aesthetically. This would raise problems enough if it were a matter of somatic therapy, affecting only a consenting individual. But one can also anticipate such questions arising in relation to germ-line therapy, which will affect the individual's descendants. Then the problems will be infinitely greater.

I will just indicate a number of points that strike me about the moral implications of that kind of choice.

The first is that germ-line therapy has a potentially uncontrollable effect on future generations. After a couple of generations, if some adverse effect emerged, it might not even be possible to trace all the descendants of the person with the altered gene. The damage might be very difficult or impossible to undo. Even when germ-line therapy is administered to eliminate a fatal disease, any adverse effects may strike even those descendants who have not inherited the disease. Experiments on animals have so far shown that germ-line therapy involves high levels of morbidity and mortality on embryos subjected to it.[27]

Secondly, we need to ask whether we know as much as we think we do about the human genome. Even if one can establish that a particular gene has a particular effect, how sure can we be that this is its only effect? Are we sure that genes operate only as individual switches, or might they also operate in a virtually unlimited series of combinations with each other?

Thirdly, we should not be too quick to assume that we know what would count as 'perfecting' the human person. I remember hearing about a fire in a residential home in which there were a number of disturbed and occasionally aggressive children. As soon as they saw the fire, these little lads ran to the store room, soaked blankets, threw them over their heads and ran into the building to rescue the people still inside. They succeeded in saving everyone. It struck me that, if someone had removed their gene for aggression and assertiveness, and replaced them with genes for responsibility and prudence, they would have stood there and done nothing! The aggressive person may be the person who can survive in a crisis or take control in an emergency. It would be foolhardy to try to make everyone into the kind of person with whom we would feel comfortable. If we succeeded, the human race would be in trouble if global warming or some disaster were to bring about a situation that would require skills and traits that we do not have much use for. There is always, as I said, a temptation to the arrogant assumption that one's own cultural perspective is the only possible one!

Most importantly, we will have to ask ourselves this fundamental question. How can we reconcile this newfound knowledge and ability with seeing human life as a gift of God?

If we are offered the possibility of changing the appearance and the personality of future generations, how can we avoid buying into the idea of the human being as a machine to be produced and redesigned according to our whims? At what point might we radically alter the genetic makeup so that the question would arise as to whether what was produced was a member of the human family?

We can already see on the not too distant horizon the prospect of a cloned human being. We have already heard the warnings from the Roslin Institute about the irresponsibility of such an undertaking, given the uncertainties and the failure rate of the procedures they have pioneered.

Even if the technique were foolproof, there would be horrendous moral implications. Having produced a human being for the precise purpose of being identical to someone else, how could that person have the freedom to be him or herself? How could we resist the temptation to see the cloned person as a product of our ingenuity rather than as the gift of God?

There are many different kinds of scientific intervention in the process of human generation. If one sees the human being as a machine and procreation as a technical process of bringing sperm and ovum together and providing a suitable setting for the development of an embryo, it will not matter greatly what technique is used. The concern will be for effectiveness.

If one looks rather at the mystery of how a new member of the human family is called into existence by God, the matter will appear differently. Procreation is meant to occur in the context of a conjugal act; it is not a manufacturing process but a fruitful relationship:

> The status of the child as 'begotten not made' is assured by the fact that she is not the primary object of attention in that embrace which gave her her being. In that embrace the primary object of attention to each partner is the other. The I-Thou predominates.

> The She (or He) which will spring from the I-Thou is always present as a possibility, but never as project pure and simple. And precisely for that reason she cannot be demeaned to the status of an artefact, a product of the will.[28]

The human person is meant to come into existence in an act of self-giving and permanently committed love, not as the product of medical or biological techniques. Procreation occurs in the meeting of persons, not just in the combination of gametes. The result of procreation is not merely a fertilised ovum but a being brought into existence by God and loved for his or her own sake:

> The human person must be accepted in his/her parents' act of union and love: the generation of a child must therefore be the fruit of that mutual giving which is realised in the conjugal act through which the spouses cooperate as servants not as masters in the work of the Creator who is love.[29]

Every human 'I' comes into existence in the context of the 'we' of his or her parents, and in a wider sense the context of the 'we' of his or her grandparents and relatives and the context of the 'we' of the whole human family. That is the context that techniques of artificial fertilisation distort, even when the biological parents of the child are married and will accept their child with love and gratitude to God.

Much more unacceptable would be the production of a cloned human being who would have no parents but only a human template, an adult 'twin', who wishes for some reason to bring into existence a younger replica of him or herself.

A contemplative outlook

The vision of human dignity which underlies what I have been saying does not reveal itself to a superficial glance. It requires reflection on the meaning and purpose of life and a sense of the mystery of the human being – an embodied spirit, an infinite longing in a limited universe, a soaring search for truth and beauty and moral nobility in the context of imperfect knowledge, flawed creativity and moral frailty.

That is why the Pope tells us that to appreciate and celebrate the Gospel of Life we need to foster in ourselves and in others what he calls 'a contemplative outlook':

> It is the outlook of those who see life in its deeper meaning, who grasp its utter gratuitousness, its beauty and its invitation to freedom and responsibility. It is the outlook of those who do not presume to take possession of reality but instead accept it as a gift, discovering in all things the reflection of the Creator and seeing in every person the Creator's living image. This outlook does not give in to discouragement when confronted by those who are sick, suffering, outcast or at death's door. Instead, in all these situations it feels challenged to find meaning, and precisely in these circumstances it is open to perceiving in the face of every person a call to encounter, dialogue and solidarity.[30]

He goes on to make it clear that this is not a call directed simply to religious and clergy. It is a call to 'all of us... to rediscover the ability to revere and honour every person'. Perhaps it is surprising, as we face such practical problems from abortion to genetic manipulation, that we find ourselves called to contemplation.

The surprise we may feel, however, may simply indicate the depth of our need to recognise that life is a mystery. The

Pope is issuing a call to renew our sense of awe and wonder in the face of God's gift of human life. The response to that call will face us with the most demanding practical implications of building a new culture of life and solidarity. We will face those demands by no means least in the field of health care.

Notes
1. John Paul II, *Evangelium vitae (EV)*, 8.
2. *EV*, 12.
3. *Catechism of the Catholic Church*, 366.
4. Vatican II, *Gaudium et spes* 24.
5. *EV*, 2, cf. *GS* 45.
6. R. Spaemann, 'On the anthropology of the Encyclical *Evangelium vitae*', in *Evangelium vitae*, Pontificia Academia pro Vita, Libreria Editrice Vaticana 2001, p. 446.
7. *Gaudium et spes*, 24.
8. John Paul II, *Sollicitudo rei socialis*, 40.
9. *EV*, 81.
10. *EV*, 75.
11. *EV*, 76.
12. *EV*, 19.
13. Pontifical Council for the Instruments of Social Communication, *Communio et progressio* (1971), 11.
14. Vatican II, *Lumen gentium*, 9.
15. cf. *Gaudium et spes* 24.
16. *EV*, 43.
17. *EV*, 81.
18. *EV*, 81.
19. P. Marchesi, 'The medical world in suspense', in *Dolentium hominum (DH)* n.1, Vatican 1986, p. 15.
20. John Paul II, to the Conference on the Humanisation of Medicine, *Osservatore Romano* (English edition), 7 December 1987.
21. P. Marchesi, 'To effect change...' in *DH* n.7, Vatican 1988, pp. 107, 108.
22. *EV*, 2.
23. *EV*, 81.

24. *EV*, 53.
25. *EV*, 62, 65.
26. Congregation for the Doctring of the Faith, *Declaration on Procured Abortion* (1974), 12.
27. The Catholic Bishops' Joint Committee on Bioethical Issues, *Genetic Intervention on Human Subjects*, London 1996, p. 33.
28. O. O'Donovan, *Begotten or Made?*, Clarendon Press 1984, p. 17.
29. Congregation for the Doctring of the Faith, *Donum vitae* B, 4, c.
30. *EV*, 83.